The Explanation of Behavior: A Control Theory of Everything

I0436639

ISBN 9781534612693

Library of Congress Control Number: 2016916128
CreateSpace Independent Publishing Platform, North Charleston, SC

www.DrLuisGuerreiro.com

Ψ SCS — Statewide Clinical Services, LLC

P. O. Box 5247
Newark, New Jersey 07105

The Explanation of Behavior: A Control Theory of Everything

THE
EXPLANATION
OF
BEHAVIOR

A Control Theory
of
Everything

Luis A. Guerreiro, Psy. D.

ABOUT THE AUTHOR

Dr. Luis A. Guerreiro is a licensed psychologist practicing clinical, school, and consulting psychology. He was a fellow at the New York University Medical Center in New York City in the late 1980s and earned his doctoral degree from the prestigious Graduate School of Applied and Professional Psychology (GSAPP), Rutgers University at New Brunswick, New Jersey, in 1989. He has made professional contributions to Children's Specialized Hospital, Newark Public Schools, and several other public and private school systems and agencies in New Jersey, where he has been practicing since 1992.

For about a year, in 1989-1990, Dr. Guerreiro opened and maintained a small clinical practice in Algarve, Portugal, where he also created and produced a weekly radio talk show with live listeners calling in to consult on issues of psychology and mental health. During that period he became a member of APPORT, a Portuguese association of professional psychologists, which preceded the current Ordem dos Psicólogos.

He has published professional articles in refereed journals on both sides of the Atlantic, namely in *Contemporary Education* and *Jornal de Psicologia*. Dr. Guerreiro was for several years on the editorial board of *Special Services in the Schools*, a quarterly journal published as a platform and resource for psychologists working in educational environments.

Dr. Guerreiro speaks and practices in English, Portuguese, and Spanish, which has given him the opportunity to work with a diversity of multiethnic and multicultural populations. To a great extent, this diversity in professional experience has helped him deepen his views and understanding of how individuals, groups, families, and organizations function and evolve.

Little known to many who know him professionally, Dr. Guerreiro has also been, in the course of his multifaceted life and career, a journalist, published poet, radio personality, and writer of political commentary and fictional stories.

Dr. Guerreiro has two biological daughters, three stepdaughters, and a growing number of grandchildren. He lives with his wife in the Delaware River Valley.

The Explanation of Behavior: A Control Theory of Everything

PREFACE

On the surface, this is one more book in the vast ocean of the printed word. I am certain, though, that this one book will help you expand your way of looking at the world around you and within you. The burdens and challenges of life will seem to make more sense once you look at them in this new way. I made a deliberate effort to keep my message simple and as entertaining as I could, since I know well that no one wants to read a boring book.

This is not a book for just psychologists. It is a book for anyone who is curious to know about human nature and what makes us tick. So, relax, grab a glass of water, sit in your favorite spot, and begin your journey into the space of day-to-day psychology. If you feel the text gets a little too serious sometimes, or too profound in its discourse, do not get discouraged. This is, after all, a book about serious stuff.

Throughout the text I use anecdotes to illustrate certain points. Although such illustrations are mostly based on and abstracted from my clinical experience working with thousands of patients and school kids over a period of three decades, I made sure, in every instance, that names, locations, family constellations, gender, or other identifying data were changed to protect the identity of those who inspired me. If any names or situations   bear any similarity to real people or situations you may know, such resemblance is merely coincidental.

Some aspects of the theory and ideas in this book can potentially ignite or fuel strong reactions or controversy. I can only say that I do speak my mind and don't bow to pressure from "power" (you will know more about power when you read chapter 7). I value independence of thought as much as I appreciate clean water, fresh air, a bottle of good wine, the love of my family, and the friendship of so many of you I have met already and others I will get to know in the future. I am not a "communist," a socialist, a mason, a capitalist, or a conspiracy theorist. Like you, I am perhaps a little of all of the above. But, for the record, I do value clarity and openness over obscurantism, secrecy, and malicious manipulation of the facts of life. I value cooperation over competition; altruism over egotism, selfishness, and greed; conserving, saving and recycling over wasting, ruining, and destroying; and I definitely value peace over aggression, violence, and war.

While reviewing the text, I was struck by certain key words that seem to underscore the purpose of the book. For example, the word *you* is the connective thread throughout the text. It sets the tone of the writing. It commutes the ideas from here to there. It brings spirit and life into each paragraph. As I write the words I can imagine you reading them. This book is meant to be an interactive process that goes beyond you and me. I am very interested   in knowing what you think of the concepts and ideas addressed in the book.

The Explanation of Behavior: A Control Theory of Everything

Do not hesitate to drop me a note with your thoughts or comments. You can e-mail me at luisguerreiro@DrLuisGuerreiro.com.

This is a book for all who can appreciate the paradoxical aspects of life. It is for you to learn more about yourself and about the people who sit next to you on the ride through the eternal flow of the Universe. Remember that life is a one-way journey. This book will hopefully help you prepare for the rest of your journey. Take it as a road map from someone who *travels* a lot and has been there. Have fun!

Luis A. Guerreiro, Psy.D.
October, 2016

The Explanation of Behavior: A Control Theory of Everything

This book is dedicated to:

My wife, Vicky,
my ex-wife, Maria de Lasalete,
our children,
Jennifer,
Ana-Sophia,
Jacqueline,
Ivid,
and Janelle
(all grown up now),
who, each in their own way, gave me love, inspiration,
and motivation during the thirty years it took me to
write this book.

ACKNOWLEDGEMENTS

I want to thank all of you who, possibly unknowingly, helped me along the way to put my ideas together and provided me with resources, information, data, and support.

Some of you read parts of the manuscript as I asked for your feedback and comments. Others patiently listened to and watched the improvised presentations and demonstrations of my theory. Yet others actively argued with me in an effort to prove me wrong. It is impossible to mention you all by name.

I am especially grateful to Ivid Arguello-Brea, Marcia Alvarez, Jean Balinly, Christopher Barbrack, Ana-Sophia Cohen, Albert E. Goss, Maria V. Lopez-Guerreiro, Ricardo Gil, Charles A. Maher, Jeffrey Ruttner, Milton Schwebel, Kenneth Schneider, and Scott Wolfenden. Some of you are no longer with us, but you will forever live in my memory and on the pages of this book.

I wholeheartedly thank you all, hoping I have not let you down.

Luis A. Guerreiro, Psy.D.

TABLE OF CONTENTS

The Explanation of Behavior: A Control Theory of Everything

The Explanation of Behavior: A Control Theory of Everything

Chapter 6: The Future of Human Behavior (176)

Introduction (177)

The Future of Human Behavior (177)

> How History Relates to the Future of
> Behavior (178)
>
> The Two Phases of Human Social Evolution
> (179)
>> Phase One: Selfishness and Prejudice
>> (179)
>> Phase Two: Altruism and
>> Cooperativism (182)
>
> Redefinition of Values in the Future (185)
>> A New Form of Rationalization (186)
>> Energy of the Future (187)
>> Democracy of the Future (188)
>> Role of the Government in the
>> Future (190)
>> Privacy of the Future (190)
>> Universal Bill of Human Rights (191)

Conclusion (195)

Chapter 7: The Future and Control Dynamics (197)

Introduction (198)

The Explanation of Behavior: A Control Theory of Everything

The Explanation of Behavior: A Control Theory of Everything

Chapter 1

Understanding Yourself and Others: A Brief Overview

of

Psychology

The Explanation of Behavior: A Control Theory of Everything

INTRODUCTION

Politics, education, and psychology are subjects everyone knows something about.   Talk instead about hunting, Einstein's theory of relativity, or the greenhouse effect and most people will suddenly become quiet around the table, due to subtle and polite philosophical disagreements or because of self-admitted ignorance of the subject matter. But ask how was it possible that George W. Bush was re-elected for a second term in office, how can we explain to ourselves or to the world that (out of over 300 million Americans) we end up with Hilary Clinton and Donald Trump as our best choices for president, how come "Johnny" is not doing well in school, or why such and such missed her high-school reunion two nights ago -- and every person at the table will have something to say.

Why is it that we think we know so much about ourselves, and yet we really know so little? In part at least, I believe that the reason why practical psychology seems to be such an apparently *easy* subject to so many is because each of us carries within ourselves the entire *code* that would indeed make it possible to understand the inner secrets of the *mind*. But we have not found the sequence of that code, more or less the same way our genes used to hide in the continuous flux of the DNA helix, prior to the mapping of the human genome. We know we have the answers, but they are as elusive as our own shadows. And, in spite of everyone's quick guesses and opinions, the *process of knowing* about human behavior has been and continues to be laborious and slow.

The question is: Do you really know what you are talking about whenever you say this or that about yourself or someone else? You probably do know if you want to be absolutely honest about your own instincts and motivations. Most of the time, however, you prefer not to know what your mind is about. Most of the time people play disguising tricks, in their own minds, in order to cope with the world around. The tricks themselves are part of the code necessary to understand the mind.

The purpose of this chapter is to give you a general overview of psychology and its recent history while in the context of reviewing the scientific method and its implications on what we think we know and how we know. I will also summarize, in very simple terms, the most popular theories of psychology-personality-behavior-motivation. This will bring to the surface facts about psychology you may have learned before and will also give you some food for thought in the process of *helping you understand why people behave in the way they do.* **It will also prepare you for the chapters that follow.**

The Explanation of Behavior: A Control Theory of Everything

PSYCHOLOGY AS A SCIENCE (OR IS IT AN ART?)

Psychology is a relatively new science. It didn't exist, as we know it today, only a little more than a century ago. For many centuries, psychology was an obscure part of philosophy, which is often considered to be a "residual" discipline, since philosophy covers all those aspects of Man's relationship with the rest of the Universe not addressed in the other branches of science.

Because of its loosely defined scope, philosophy has its doors open to the unknown, the magical, the spiritual, the reasonable and the unreasonable. You find in philosophy, side by side, mysticism and logic, the supernatural and the psychological. It is a field wide open to speculation. Yet, long before the independence of America or the beginning of the French revolution, you find someone like Thomas Hobbes (Levy, 1954), a seventeenth century British philosopher who wrote the ground rules for what would become the moral social contract, which the French philosopher Jean-Jacques Rousseau further developed and promoted in the eighteenth century and modern *democratic* nations still struggle to live by today. Hobbes understood better than most in his time that the relationship between the civil society and the state must follow certain moral expectations and responsibilities and that the state must be representative of the people.

Psychology's breaking away from philosophy during the latter part of the nineteenth century was therefore a rather important event in its own history.   It freed itself from the burdens of politics, magic, and witchcraft, and became a science.

The Birth of Psychology as a Science

The birth of psychology as a scientific discipline is usually associated with the name of Wilhelm Max Wundt, a German philosophy professor who offered the first academic course in psychology in 1862. He emphasized "observation" of the conscious mind, rather than "inference." Considering that reliable observation is the mother of all sciences, Wundt's publication of *Principles of Physiological Psychology* around 1874 (Wundt, 1910) opened the front door of Science to what, in my opinion, continues to be the most unexplored, misunderstood, fascinating, and yet eluding branch of knowledge of all times, past and future. In what is considered to have been the first known psychology laboratory, Wundt studied sensation and perception, functions at the very core of all psychological phenomena. In fact, sensation and perception provide the bridge between physiology and psychology.

Russian physiologist Ivan Pavlov further established psychology as a serious science with his classical experimental research in the areas of conditioned and unconditioned reflexes in dogs, beginning in or about 1889 (Asratyan, 1953). In the United States, it was William James' publication of *The Principles of Psychology* in 1890 promoting his ideas on "functionalism" in psychology that marks the spot of psychology's grand entrance into the halls of science.

Freud and Psychoanalysis

Interestingly, at about the same time Pavlov was toying around with his dogs, another famous doctor, Sigmund Freud, was stirring waves of controversy with his brand new approach to the understanding of the human mind, which became known as *psychoanalysis* in 1896 (Freud, 1896). The interesting part in all this comes from the fact that while Wundt, Pavlov, and others were going out of their way to make psychology an *exact* science, one that relies on objective measurement of psychological phenomena, Freud's psychoanalysis relied on *inferences* associated with unknown concepts such as the "unconscious," the "ego," the "superego," and the "id," which scientists vehemently questioned, considering that the existence of these concepts could not be objectively observed, demonstrated, or documented.

To this date, psychoanalytic theory remains a highly controversial facet of psychology. But Freud made his point and came to be considered, even by those who disagree with his ideas, one of the most notable minds of modern times.

Psychoanalysis vs. Behaviorism

With the appearance of Freud's work, the then still very young and tender discipline of psychology became forever split into two main camps. On one side is Freud with his psychoanalysis and a number of its subsequent variations and

The Explanation of Behavior: A Control Theory of Everything

adaptations making their ways into the clinical setting as well as into literature, the arts, and almost every other aspect of our culture. On the other side is Pavlov and his salivating dogs, followed by several equally notable psychologists, like John Watson (1930), B. F. Skinner (1938), Joseph Wolpe (1969), and Hans Eysink (1964)--to name only the most famous ones who truly brought psychology into the respectful pinnacle of scientific rigor, under a brand of psychology generally known as *behaviorism*, a psychological current that became very popular in the U.S.A. during the first half of the twentieth century.

The truth is that these two different perspectives and a large number of variations and combinations of psychological theories (or personality theories, as they are commonly called in psychological jargon) are in fact mere different geographical points on the surface of the same sphere---the understanding of psychology is far more complex than the proverbial flat and linear two-sided coin.

Psychology, science or not, is deep enough to comprehend, integrate, and absorb all that has been done, said, and written about it, and the much more that is still to come. I think that psychology is so deep that in these past one hundred fifty years or so, we have done little more than scratch its surface here and there.

In spite of the serious competition posed by behaviorists, Freud and his many followers managed to plant the seed that would raise a question many people still entertain today: *Is Psychology a science, or is it really an art?* Of course, the obvious answer it that it is both and much more! But, believe it or not, some of my otherwise rational psychologist colleagues will still take issue and argue very seriously over this point.

Third Forces in Psychology

In addition to psychoanalysis and behaviorism, other influential brands of personality theory are *humanism, social learning theory, cognitive theory, systems theory, perceptual control theory, choice theory*, and *information processing* theories. There are, as stated above, many combinations of these theories, the best known being the so called *cognitive-behavioral theory*, very much used as a successful intervention framework in contemporary psychotherapy and other clinical applications. In recent decades, William Glasser's *reality therapy* (1965) and *choice theory* (1998) have become popular, in what I call the "I" society. Choice theory, unlike Dr. Powers' *perceptual control theory* (Powers, 1973) on which it may have been inspired, emphasizes the responsibility of the individual on *selecting the behavior* (making the choice) rather that the potential parameters established and determined by the environment in which the individual was "programmed" (the individual's belief system and experiential and knowledge base).

So, without boring you to death, let me explain the highlights of each of these theories. Before doing that, however, I must jump outside of the frame myself, and I must create a context, or an environment, where each of these theories makes sense in its own way. I will review very briefly what the world has come to accept as *the scientific method* and how psychology fits into that model.

What is Psychology, After All?

Psychology is the scientific study of behavior and experience in humans and other animals. It is also the study of how humans and animals sense, perceive, think, learn, feel, and know about self and about the world around them.

While studying the behavior of pigeons in a laboratory is a relatively straightforward task, studying how humans think, feel, learn, and know is somewhat more difficult. If you have ever tried to give yourself a hair cut, you probably understand what I am saying. It is cumbersome to study yourself. It can be done, but it requires a great deal of openness, honesty, and courage on your part. I believe that this awkwardness is the main reason why psychology, the science that studies our own "head," has progressed at such a slow rate, in scientific terms, when compared to other sciences such as physics or chemistry.

SCIENCE AND THE SCIENTIFIC METHOD

Since the word "science" keeps popping up, I must explain what it means, without, of course, insulting your intelligence. Even though you most likely already know what the scientific method is about, I still recommend that you do not skip this section, as subsequent sections of the book will refer to the anecdotes used here.

The Explanation of Behavior: A Control Theory of Everything

What is Science?

Science, or the scientific method, is one way of knowing about something. There are other ways of knowing, but the other ways tend to be less objective and less reliable. When talking among themselves, scientists use the word "epistemology" instead of saying "a way of knowing." Religious belief, science, superstition, random guessing, and intuition are all different ways of knowing about something, and can be considered epistemological approaches.

If you were planning to travel in the Gulf of Mexico during the month of September, which of the above epistemological approaches would you prefer to rely on in order to anticipate the possibility of a hurricane coming your way? It really depends on who you are, but I can assure you that most people I know would definitely prefer science to let them know whether it would be safe to cross the Gulf of Mexico on a given day in September.

Rationale for the Scientific Method

So, what is it about science that makes it so serious, so reliable, and, therefore, so desirable? A science is, after all, the refined result of a long-term process of methodical experimentation and collecting of observations. All sciences were established around the need to *understand*, *predict*, and *control* a given class of often naturally occurring phenomena. It is very unlikely that a science begins and establishes itself as a perfect package of concepts or ideas suddenly appearing in the radar of human curiosity. There are usually a lot of false starts and failures before a scientific accomplishment makes its way to the podium.

The evolutionary process of a science is often expected to begin with a question, or set of questions, or a problem, or set of problems. For example, one can only imagine the emotions experienced by our pre-historic ancestors each time they witnessed lightening striking a nearby tree and setting it on fire. The questions and the *need to know* arising from such frightening events may have set the stage which, many thousands of years later, led to the understanding, predicting, and controlling of what we call electricity, something we seem not to be able to live without today.

The Questions of Science

Scientists ask questions such as *what, where, when, how,* and *why,* and also *how much, how many, how long, how frequently,* and *with what intensity?* These questions will lead to theories.

What is a Theory? One theory may be very different from other theories, but they all attempt to explain the underlying rules and regularities that guide the occurrence of a specific phenomenon, often long before one has the means or the technology to prove or disprove one's theory.

Theories are the force and the motivation behind all intentional scientific efforts. America was "discovered" by Christopher Columbus not because he rolled the dice and the dice read "Travel West," but because he had a *theory* and he wanted to prove that his theory was right. Since airplanes did not exist at the time, the only way to prove that the earth is round (the theory) was setting sail towards West and arriving at the same point coming from the East. Historically, it appears that Columbus may have been more interested in the financial results of his voyage than in its scientific significance. Regardless of his true agenda, hadn't he bumped into America, his "theory" would have been proven.

Since the obstruction posed by the American continent did not allow confirmation of the roundness of the earth (although Columbus himself apparently never knew that, as he thought he had reached the Asian continent), it was the Portuguese navigator Fernão de Magalhães (Ferdinand Magellan) who went out to sea to set the record straight on that burning question. Unfortunately, Magellan was killed by natives in the Philippines, and we don't know for sure whether or not he knew, before he died, that he had actually accomplished most of the job. The glory was enjoyed by his traveling partner, Juan Sebastián Elcano, the Spaniard who completed the first trip around the Earth ever and arrived in Spain not from the East (there was no Suez Canal at the time), but from the South, which meant the same, on September 6, 1522.

Though with a lot of unanswered questions left on the workbench of science for the future to solve, the theory of the "roundness of the Earth" was proven. A theory is not more than that until it can be proved or disproved. Magellan devised an *experiment*--his voyage-- with the purpose of proving or disproving a theory—the round nature of the Earth.

What is a Hypothesis? In a true scientific experiment, the scientist must state a *hypothesis* before he or she begins the experiment. So what is a hypothesis? A hypothesis is simply a statement that predicts a certain result or outcome for a specific experiment. *A hypothesis can be defined as an anticipated answer to the question the experiment is designed to answer. Or, in simpler terms, a hypothesis states the guess of the scientist doing the experiment.* Ironically, a hypothesis is often stated in the negative, and it is called the *null hypothesis*. Therefore, scientists are in the business of confirming or not their own null hypotheses.

Steps in the Scientific Method

In Magellan's case, the scientific method may be outlined as follows:

Broad question
--*What is the shape of the Earth?*

Theory (triggered by the broad question)
--*The earth is round* (still an unproven concept at the time);

Experiment (designed to prove or disprove the theory)
--*Sail straight from Spain, going West (circumventing America from the South);*

Hypothesis (Null Hypothesis)

-- A navigator sailing past the American continent   traveling West will not arrive in Europe from the South contouring the West coast of Africa;

Results
--Magellan's null hypothesis was not confirmed, thus **proving** *his (and others') theory that* **the Earth is round;**

Conclusion
--Since Magellan's experiment can be duplicated and the results will not change (in science this is called *reliability*), **it is now a scientific fact that the Earth is round**.

This very simplified outline of the scientific method is a universal framework used by scientists in most branches of science, including the Science of Psychology. However, as we will see, the nature of psychology makes it very difficult for the scientist to prove or disprove theories.

PERSONALITY THEORIES

What are the broad questions posed to the psychologist? Well, how about, *Why does a mother place her own infant daughter in a hot oven to die?* Or *Why does one man intentionally kill another man to steal five dollars from his wallet? Why does a dog salivate when he smells food? Why does a man jump into a frozen river and risks his own life to save the life of a total stranger? Why do people work? Why do some people smoke? Why do we fall in love?* The questions could go on, and on, and on... But I believe that they all can be synthesized in one simple grand question: ***Why do people behave the way they do when they do?*** In other words, what motivates people to do all the things they do all the time? Unfortunately, psychological theories tend to address only parts and bits of the grand question, and not the whole question.

Questions beginning with *"why"* are the most difficult to answer. They address overall underlying motivational forces, which supposedly determine behavior in organisms, including humans. *"What, when,* and *how* questions are easier to answer because they tend to represent more circumscribed, more tightly definable, and more environmentally (externally) based research problems.

In the last one hundred years, psychologists have advanced a large number of theories addressing a broad range of psychological questions. The ones that address *why* questions are called personality theories, as mentioned before. I prefer to call them theories of motivation, fully knowing that Bernard Weiner (1973), who, back in the day, literally wrote the book on this subject, would have frowned at the idea of considering personality theory and motivation theory interchangeable concepts, even though he too couldn't keep them apart as he wrote about both.

You probably know or have heard how Freud's *psychoanalysis* originally placed a lot of weight on sexuality as a motivator. Freud was certainly aware of Charles Darwin's work on genetics and evolution as it relates to humans (1896) and he understood that the *instinct* to reproduce was at the base of all *instincts* underlying motivation, the *id*, which compels people to behave. He adopted the word *libido* to describe a person's sexual *instinct* and sexual energy (sex drive). Freud also believed that the libido is often rerouted and disguised as the expression of artistic creation and other respectable human activity, which he called *sublimation*.

Behaviorism

Behaviorism rejects altogether the need to answer "why" questions. Behavioral psychologists operate under the assumption that there is no way we can "observe" with objectivity what goes on inside the person's mind. In fact, radical behaviorists question the very existence of a *mind*. They believe there is no use in even attempting to explain *why* a certain behavior occurs. Behaviorists compare the human "mind" to a "black box" where you can see what gets in and what gets out, but not what happens inside.

As scientists, behavioral psychologists are in the business of rigorously observing and recording what gets *in* and what gets *out*, and then run statistical analyses on the relationships between these two sets of paired observations. The behavioral psychologist looks for patterns involving behavior and environmental events. Once such patterns are reliably established over time, the psychologist can be fairly sure that certain environmental events (*stimuli*) are "associated" with certain behaviors (*responses*).

<u>*Classical Conditioning*</u>. The stimulus-response model (or *paradigm*) was sufficient to explain reflexive behavior. For example, every time a hungry dog smells food (the stimulus), the dog then salivates (the response). It is very simple, and it literally *almost* doesn't require a brain, as we know it. Every time the neurologist taps on your knee (the stimulus), your leg jerks up (the response). Although technically these two examples represent two different types of stimulus-response relationships, due to the "wiring" of the nerve cells involved in each of the two processes, these examples do share the fact that the organism (the dog or the person) does not have a choice on whether or not to respond in a certain way--The response is said to be involuntary.

From a scientific point of view, the scientist can safely conclude that *there is a strong and reliable relationship between the smell of food (what goes in) and salivation (what comes out) in dogs.* By the same token, the scientist concludes *that there is a strong and reliable relationship between knee tapping (what goes in) and leg jerking (what comes out).*

In psychology, since most scientific phenomena cannot be observed directly, scientists avoid to say that one event *causes* another event. Explanation of psychological scientific results in terms of causality is tricky and potentially harmful (especially in attempting to explain human behavior), particularly because there are so many potential factors involved in the simplest of behaviors, as we will see.

A true scientist never claims more than what he or she can soundly explain in the light of the available data. In the context of the two examples above, it would be acceptable to say that knee tapping *causes* leg jerking in humans, because we know now that such a response is instinctive, totally involuntary, and requires no learning at all (this kind of reflexive response is genetically programmed in the person by the time the person is born). However, it would not be appropriate to say that the smell of food *causes* salivation in dogs. I can imagine your brow raised as you read this and ask "But... Isn't the dog born already programmed to salivate when smelling food?" The answer is "Yes," and "No"...

I'm certain that you have or had a dog at some point in your life or remember some dog that you had the chance to know closely. Let's name that dog "Pilot." Let's assume that you own Pilot and you own Pilot's mother as well. So you know Pilot since birth. In fact you nurtured Pilot's mother all through her pregnancy. To make sure that the little dogs would be born healthy, you fed the mother only food of the brand X. You feed her with food X everyday. X has a rich, characteristic smell that fills the room as soon as you open the can.

When Pilot is born, he feeds on his mother's milk. But the smell of what the mother eats is all over the place. And, sure enough, little Pilot will soon be eating the same food that the mother eats.

The Explanation of Behavior: A Control Theory of Everything

He develops a *liking* for food X, because that is what he has *available* and what meets his physiological needs. So, now, when you arrive home at the end of the day and open a can of food X, Pilot begins to salivate as soon as the smell of X fills the room. Pilot has learned to recognize (*discriminate*) the smell of food X amongst all smells available to him.

One day you run out of food X and open a can of food Z. This is totally new for Pilot, who has never *experienced* this smell, and he will not recognize this as *food*. He has not *learned* that smelling Z means food in the mouth really soon.

As opposed to the leg jerking example, which involves a totally inborn mechanism, the salivating-dog example requires a *learning process* before the stimulus-response relationship can be established.

Now, let's get real here and let's not kid ourselves! If you know anything about dogs, you are saying that this is all nonsense. Everybody knows that the dog will begin salivating as soon as he can hear your car coming half a mile away. He is not going to wait until you open the can, smell the food, and then salivate... So, what's going on? Well, well... This is exactly why, in psychology, the scientist must refrain from saying that *this stimulus causes that response*. Since the dog can learn by means of associating different stimuli occurring simultaneously or in a certain sequence in time or proximity in space, to say that the smell of food *causes* the dog to salivate would not be correct. The same *intelligence* that made it possible for

The Explanation of Behavior: A Control Theory of Everything

Pilot to know that the smell of food X means soon to be food in his mouth, made it possible for him to know that hearing your car at a distance, seeing you come through the door, or the sight of your briefcase, means smell of food X soon to fill the air.

In his classical experiments, Pavlov may have become bored with his *sight-of-food* straight to *salivation* results, and he began to play around with new experimental designs. So one thing he did was to ring a bell just before he presented the food to the dog. Sure enough, he found what we, *of course*, already know. He found that after a few times of the *bell-food-salivation* sequence, the dog would salivate anyway, even if the food were not present. The ringing of the bell alone was sufficient to make the dog salivate, even when food was nowhere near to be smelled, seen, or eaten!

Bingo! Pavlov had just made one of his most important contributions to the science of psychology. Pavlov had *proven* in a very simple way that organisms can learn to *generalize* characteristics of one stimulus onto another stimulus, even though the new stimulus may be completely unrelated and potentially independent from the original stimulus, as long as the two stimuli remain closely associated in *time* or in *space*. Pavlov called the bell ring (this reoccurring, yet circumstantial stimulus) the *conditioned* stimulus--a stimulus that is not a stimulus until *conditioned* to be perceived as such. By the same token, he named the response elicited by such a stimulus (salivation without the presence of food) *conditioned response*. And from then on it became fashionable to say that this or that person has been conditioned to display this or that behavior. Conditioning became particularly interesting when it was clear that it applied to humans as well as to other animals and that it could actually be used in clinical settings for the treatment of anxiety and undesirable habits.

Let's consider this other example. A baby is crying, and crying, and crying... A behaviorist observing the baby rather then asking *why* is the baby crying, will ask *what* appears to make the baby cry? Or, *what* will likely make him stop? The baby is held and gently rocked for five minutes (this *treatment* is what *goes in*--the stimulus). The baby stops crying (this *decrease in crying* would be what *comes out*--the response). This simple observation would give the behavioral psychologist interesting material for a research hypothesis, namely that *holding and gentle rocking decreases crying in babies.* This is not yet a scientific fact. It is merely his or her hypothesis.

So the psychologist designs an experiment to confirm (or not) this hypothesis. The psychologist looks for confirmation in large numbers. He randomly selects one thousand babies from a population of available crying babies. The psychologist randomly divides these babies in two equivalent groups of five hundred babies. One is called the experimental group and the other is called the control group. For all that matters, these two groups of crying babies are alike, the only difference being that the babies in the experimental group will be held and gently rocked for five minutes while *nothing* will be done to the babies in the control group.

At the end of five minutes, the number of babies who are not crying is counted in each of the two groups. Let's suppose that all babies in the control group continue to cry after the five minutes have passed, while 95% of the babies in the experimental group have stopped crying. These results would lead the psychologist to conclude that holding and gentle rocking does indeed reduce the frequency of crying in babies--*now a scientific fact* after completion of this hypothetical experiment. Note that the behavioral psychologist reaches this conclusion without dwelling on the issue of *why* holding and gentle rocking reduces frequency of crying in babies. In the same way that Pavlov did not dwell much on *why* did the dogs salivate when hearing the bell.

The whole concept can be explained in this simple paragraph: *Classical conditioning is what happens when an organism (let's say a dog, a fly, or a human being) learns to predict or to anticipate the occurrence of one event based on the occurrence of another event (or chain of events). The two (or more) events occur closely together in space and/or in time. One or more events have thus become associated with the event being anticipated or predicted.*

Step 1) Conditioned Stimulus $\Rightarrow$ Stimulus $\Rightarrow$ Response

Step 2) Conditioned Stimulus $\Rightarrow$ Conditioned Response

The Explanation of Behavior: A Control Theory of Everything

Classical conditioning acknowledges the organism's ability to use *stimulus generalization* (the ability to recognize a stimulus even when it is not exactly the same as it was experienced before) and *stimulus discrimination* (the ability to know that a stimulus is different from another experienced before even when both stimuli are very similar). Nevertheless, classical conditioning portrays the black box (the organism's brain) as a rather dumb kind of box. It assumes that the organism responds only to stimuli that are *here* and *now*. It assumes that the organism operates in a *reactive mode.* You show food and the dog salivates. You step on someone's toes and the person goes "Ouch!..." You throw a handful of corn over the sidewalk and pigeons flock towards it. Classical conditioning is O.K. to explain certain simple behaviors but it is not enough to account for higher order learning and more complex behaviors of the kind seen in humans.

<u>*Operant Conditioning*</u>. Psychologist B. F. Skinner (1938 &1953) thought about this, and he formulated what became known as *operant conditioning.* This type of conditioning introduced the concept of *reinforcement,* a cornerstone in the development of contemporary behavioral psychology. Basically, Professor Skinner hypothesized, and demonstrated through scientific studies, that *organisms can perform behaviors as responses to events that are yet to happen.* For example, a woman goes to work all week in order to get paid on Friday (*positive reinforcement*), a man takes two aspirins in order to reduce or eliminate his headache (*negative*

---

reinforcement), and a child eats all the spinach on his or her plate in order to avoid *punishment*. In all three examples, the woman, the man, and the child, had learned beforehand (most likely through experience) that working, taking aspirin, and eating the spinach would lead to the *consequences* they wanted.

This process can be summarized as follows:

Previous learning ⇒ Behavior ⇒ Consequence.

With this model, you can increase, reduce, or maintain a specific behavior simply by manipulating the consequence that follows. Try not to pay the worker two weeks in a row and guess what will happen to her "working" behavior. Replace the aspirin with placebos and tell me what will happen to the man's preference for aspirin. Or punish the child even when he or she eats the spinach and let me know if he or she will listen to you when you say, "Finish your food..."

Although operant conditioning acknowledges the organism's ability to *think* (learn, memorize, and remember) it is still limited by the "black box" concept of radical behaviorism. There must be a better way to understand, predict, and control human behavior.

Social Learning Theory

Social learning theory is yet another popular theory in the behaviorism tradition. This theory, which is very much alive among psychologists today, finds its strongest representation in the works of Albert Bandura (1966), Walter Mischel (1968), and, more recently, Terry Wilson (Wilson & O'Leary, 1980) among many others. Very simply put, social learning theory is a social explanation of *how people learn*. For Skinner, learning is the result of past personal experience. For Bandura, learning is mostly the result of seeing what happens to others.

Vicarious Learning. One does not need to get burned on a hot stove in order to learn not to touch hot stoves. A five-year old witnessing the pain and the behavior displayed by a friend who just touched a hot stove *learns* not to touch a hot stove. This type of observational learning is called *vicarious learning*.

Modeling. Social learning theorists believe that most learning that goes on as we develop into adulthood and throughout life is really vicarious in nature through a process called *modeling*. This means that the individual has learned since birth to do what he sees others do in the surrounding environment. The individual will of course tend to do more of the behaviors that are observed to lead to desirable, successful consequences than behaviors that lead to pain, discomfort, or otherwise undesirable consequences.

Social Implications. Social learning theory plays a very significant role in the understanding of violence, racism, and trends in societal values in general, especially with the advent of television, cellular phones, the internet, and other forms of mass and social communication. In a classical experiment, Bandura showed a group of young children a film where they observed children about their own age playing with a doll. Before watching the film, the children were divided in two equivalent groups. Each group saw a different version of the film. One group saw the film showing the children playing with the doll in a very nice, gentle way. The other group saw the same children playing with the same doll in a very aggressive and violent manner. Afterwards, when Bandura gave the children in both groups the opportunity to play with a doll similar to the one featured in the film, he was not surprise to observe that the children exposed to the violent version of the film played with the doll in a similar fashion, acting aggressively towards the doll, while the group that had seen the non-violent version proceeded to play in a non-violent fashion (Bandura, Ross & Ross, 1961; Bandura, A., 1965).

Although social learning theory has provided sufficient scientific evidence that children *do what they see, more so than what they are told to do*, American television and popular videogames continues to be an abundant and easily available source of programmed violence, exposing our children to all kinds of aggressive attitudes and behaviors. No wonder crime seems to be on the rise among young teenagers and pre-adolescents!

Humanism

Humanism, or humanistic psychology stemmed from the dissatisfaction of some psychologists with both psychoanalysis and behaviorism, found by many to be rigid, incomplete, or biased, missing the point about human psychology. Humanistic psychology departs from an illness-oriented model towards a *psychology of being*. It focuses on the positive aspects of human potentiality, the capacity that all human beings have to self-develop towards self-experienced happiness. It also emphasizes the uniqueness of each human being and a sense of unconditional acceptance of the individual by self and by others. Humanistic psychology is, in a way, the psychology of hope and the psychology of believing in the immense potential of human beings to "do good."

There are several brands of humanistic psychology, but the names that appear in almost every textbook are those of Carl Rogers (1971) and Abraham Maslow (1954, 1968, & 1971). They both lived and died not long ago and are portrayed by History as two gentle men who left a legacy of light and understanding over the positive aspects of the human being.

Unconditional Regard. Carl Rogers' work is known mostly for his *client-centered* therapy (Rogers, 1951), which places the client (patient), not the therapist, at the center of the therapeutic process. In my opinion, Rogers did not really develop a theory or framework of human behavior. His theoretical statement basically promoted the idea that human behavior should be taken and accepted unconditionally as it comes. Each person is different from the next and therefore it would not make sense attempting to abstract some generalized explanation of behavior. So, in therapy, the role of the therapist is to listen, nod, and reflect back to the client. The therapist must re-state what the client has said to reassure her or him that s/he is being listened to and understood. The therapist avoids making comments or passing judgment on anything the client says. Through self-understanding and unconditional support, the person will grow and develop into a happier, better-adapted individual.

    Hierarchy of Needs. Abraham Maslow, on the other hand, though focused on the person and on the person's individuality, put forth a more structured theory of personality and motivation, which addresses the *why* of behavior. Maslow believed that human beings strive for what he called *self-actualization*, a state of self-acceptance and self-approval that underlies happiness and the ability to die in peace with oneself. He became famous for his six-level *Hierarchy of Needs*, represented by a pyramid organized in horizontal layers, the basic needs being in the lower layers of the pyramid, and the less basic, more sophisticated needs being at higher levels.

    According to Maslow, there are six levels of needs every human being strives to meet, as follows:

    Level 1.   *Physiological needs* (e.g., drinking, eating, and sleeping);

    Level 2.   *Security and safety needs* (e.g., clothing and shelter);

Level 3.   *Love and belongingness needs* (e.g., stable and reciprocal interpersonal relationships and active group affiliation and participation);

Level 4.   *Competence, prestige, and esteem needs* (e.g., work, professional development, contribution to societal life, and recognition by other individuals and by society);

Level 5.   *Self-fulfillment needs* (a feeling of inner harmony and inner satisfaction that reflects the individual's relationship with the world around);

Level 6.   *Curiosity and the need to understand* (the need to improve, discover, and seek beyond; the need to challenge oneself and excel beyond what would be necessary, required, or expected).

<u>*Peak Experiences*</u>. But perhaps the most intriguing of Maslow's concepts is what he called *peak experiences*. A peak experience is a moment in time when an individual touches the tip of the pyramid, surging from within the pyramid. Examples of peak experiences are the moment when a person reaches sexual orgasm, the feelings experienced when your favorite team scores a crucial point, or the moment when you accept a Nobel Prize. Obviously, peak experiences are subjectively defined. Their meaning, content and interpretation vary from person to person, and they are cer-

tainly unsustainable, but yet necessary. A peak experience can be something as primitive as an unrepressed sneeze, a decompressing fart, or a breath full of fresh air when surfacing from a dive. It all depends on what level of the pyramid you are taking off from. As you can imagine, what is and what is not a "peak experience" can become in itself a source of passionate discussion or controversy. How can I dare, for example, to compare a basic existential fart to the extreme honor and recognition of winning a Nobel Prize?

Humanism reached a peak-popularity of its own in the U.S.A. during the nineteen sixties and seventies, and it is not a stranger to the anti-war sentiment that developed during those two decades. It continues to be a widely accepted motivation and personality theory today, but, somehow, it has not been widely applied to day-to-day life and it has not made its way into government policy. Humanism is not a formal scientific theory, as it lacks and even rejects the structure that would allow its testing via the scientific method. To my knowledge, it has not been proved or disproved in the scientific arena. Nevertheless, Maslow's concepts represent, in my opinion, the closest we have gotten to the answering of *why* questions in regard to human behavior and human psychology.

Cognitive Theory

Cognitive theory has been the driving trend in psychology since the 1950's. It is definitely my favorite approach to the understanding of human behavior, especially when combined with concepts borrowed from other theories. Why? Because cognitive psychology is finally looking inside the "black box" and trying to understand (not in psychoanalytic terms, but in scientific terms) what is going on in there.

It is fascinating! With cognitive psychology, psychologists are finally admitting that the individual has a *processing brain* and that stuff happens inside that brain that makes sense sometimes only to that one individual.

One curious aspect of all the personality theories, motivational theories, learning theories, or epistemologies, as you may like, is the fact that, like everything else in life, these different ways to look at the science of psychology are often overlapping and redundant. This happens because this is the way the world is. On the surface the world operates in a very inefficient manner, with a lot of wasting, insensitivity, and random action. In the end, however, it doesn't make a difference, as the law of conservation of matter will ensure recycling and continuity. Psychologists who come up with a new idea about how to look at psychology tend to be defectors from other camps of thinking. They break away in order to make their own individual contribution to the field of psychology. But, no matter what these defectors say, they will almost always reflect their prior ways of thinking and their prior experiences.

So, for example, some concepts of social learning theory fit perfectly into a cognitive theory model. Much of the work done by Albert Bandura, Julian Rotter, and Walter Mischel fits this *cognitive-social learning* integration.

Importance of Beliefs in Cognitive Psychology.

Cognitive psychology emphasizes the importance of what an internal or external stimulus *means* to an individual. His or her response is a function not of the stimulus itself, but of the individual's interpretation of that stimulus. Cognitive psychology assumes that the human brain is like a database of experiences, information, and knowledge accumulated through life by means of self-experience, social learning, and other forms of learning. When life presents you with a situation, your brain quickly compares the situation against *what you know* (or *believe to know*), and then *makes a decision* on *how to respond*.

Let's say that you are out in the woods one day and you realize that a tick is stuck to your skin. You look at the tick and you ask yourself what it means. It means, obviously, much more than what you can see. Your heart races, your adrenaline pumps up, you experience all kinds of scary feelings, and you go straight to your doctor, saving the tick in a little aluminum wrap, because you want to know if the tick has the virus for Lyme disease.

Now let's assume that you know nothing about Lyme disease. Would you respond the same way? Most likely you would simply brush the tick away with disgust and keep on going enjoying your walk in the woods.

When you arrive at the doctor's office, the doctor looks at the tick, smiles at you and says,

The Explanation of Behavior: A Control Theory
of Everything

"This is a soft tick, not a deer tick. Go home and relax. But I'll check the tick for you, anyway..." You feel relieved, but you also feel a bit embarrassed. How couldn't you know the difference between a soft tick and a deer tick?

In the clinical setting, cognitive psychotherapy addresses the issue of what people believe they know about themselves and about the world. Since we tend to believe what we believe we know, the individual's *beliefs* become the central targets for change in therapy. If a person is clinically depressed because she believes *no one* loves her, to change that belief becomes the goal of the therapist. Aaron Beck and Albert Ellis have revealed themselves top masters at doing this. While in graduate school, I heard interesting tales about how Dr. Ellis could "tear apart," without mercy, the strongest and most resilient maladaptive beliefs presented by his patients. He and his *rational-emotive therapy* (Ellis, 1962) became legendary worldwide. His approach focuses on debunking irrational beliefs that prevent you from reaching goals that are important to you. He does so by overemphasizing and exaggerating the very maladaptive beliefs that the client brings in. The client himself begins to feel outraged with the exaggeration and *insensitivity* of the therapist and begins to deny and de-escalate the validity and importance of the very beliefs that brought her or him in to begin with.

What is Cognition? *Cognition* means the act of knowing. So what we know helps us make sense of what we perceive around us and in ourselves, and it consequently affects how we respond. The whole concept of education is tied to this idea that we can change the world with the strength that comes from within. The expression "knowledge is power" synthesizes in three words what I just said. We believe that by *educating* our children (by giving them the opportunity to acquire knowledge) we can improve the quality of their future lives.

Systems Theory

Systems theory and different models of *information processing theory* are the riding wave of contemporary psychology. In a way, one may say that systems theory in psychology preceded the idea of globalization, which eventually permeated telephonic and wireless communications, international business, financial, cultural, and political activity, and brought about, of course, the internet.

<u>*The Advent of Cybernetics.*</u> Systems theory evolved from the work of American mathematician Norbert Wiener (1948), who, in the late 1940's, coined the term *cybernetics* to describe automated control systems in living organisms, machines, and organizations. The most significant features underlying a systems approach are:

> 1. *Circularity*--Meaning that a person's behavior impacts upon the surrounding environment, which will in turn affect the person's future behavior. This circularity may also be described as a "feedback loop."

2. *The whole is always more than the sum of its parts*--Meaning, for example, that the psychological dynamics created by a family of five members is more complex and richer than the psychology of all members when each member is considered in isolation. In psychology, as in machines, one must take into consideration the synergistic result of elements that are complementary to each other and interact amongst themselves.

3. *Self-regulation*--Meaning that the system seeks out optimal functioning and will self-adjust as needed, even at the cost of one or more of its components. Every system has its weak points. These weak points will readily *sacrifice* to save the integrity of the system. For example, every pressure system has a safety valve. If pressure rises above an optimal point, rather than keeping on rising until the system explodes, the safety valve will open and let out the excess pressure. Countries have armed forces, whose soldiers will die in war to preserve the integrity of the nation as such. Individuals are often intentionally or unintentionally used as scapegoats, as an effort to protect the integrity of a government, organization, group, or family.

The feedback loop and self-regulation are important concepts in the understanding of my ideas about behavior and will be revisited in more detail in the next chapter.

Clinical Application of Systems Theory. Systems theory has been put to use in clinical settings through family therapy. Carl Whitaker (1976), Salvador Minuchen (1974), and Jay Haley (Haley & Richeport-Haley, 2006) are examples of therapists who made family therapy one of the most popular and effective interventions to bring about change.

Rather than identifying one individual as the dysfunctional member of the family, the first task of the family therapist is to establish with all members of the family that the whole family *owns* the problem. One member may seem to be exhibiting the symptoms, but, in reality, he or she is merely acting out the role of a safety valve in the family system. Even though this approach tends to generate strong initial resistance from the system (e.g., the family), it often leads to the most robust and long lasting changes achieved by clinical intervention.

Systems psychology applications are also used in organizations and other settings with purposes such as increasing productivity, reducing and resolving conflict, and boosting morale. In broader systems, such as large and complex business organizations, countries, or geo-political regions, a systems approach is often the only viable option leading to any meaningful change or conflict resolution.

The Explanation of Behavior: A Control Theory of Everything

Perceptual Control Theory

William Powers' (1973) *Perceptual Control Theory* is by far the one framework of understanding behavior closest in focus and structure to the theory of control I am proposing in this book. As the name suggests, Powers' model emphasizes the perception aspect of control and is more specific in scope than the model I am proposing. However, both models recognize the role of perception being central to what control is to the individual, and both models share the notion of hierarchical interactive levels of control and an integration of cognitive, physiological, and neurological, as well as environmental contributing factors.

Even though the similarities are convergent (I was not familiarized with Dr. Powers work at the very early stages of my conceptualization of control theory), these two models can easily work together as a platform for research and clinical applications. What my theory exceeds in generality and reach, Perceptual Control Theory contributes in research methodology and history in the field.

Choice Theory

William Glasser's *Control Theory* (1985), which was eventually "re-labeled" *Choice Theory* (1998) is an interesting and useful framework to address human behavior within controlled settings, such as the classroom or the work environment. Unlike Powers' *Perceptual Control Theory*, Glasser's postulates that individuals have control over their own choices of behavior. It states that all human beings have five basic needs: 1) *Surviv-*

al, 2) *Love and belonging*, 3) *Power*, 4) *Freedom*, and 5) *Fun*. As individuals go through life, they make *choices* that lead to the satisfaction of these needs. I like *choice theory* for three main reasons: 1) It builds on Maslow's hierarchy of needs; 2) It is cognitive in nature, it appeals to and relies on the individual's ability to think, and 3) It recognizes the value of happiness.

However, in my opinion, choice theory can pose the following challenges: 1) It does not "protect" and "safeguard" the individual against the overwhelming circumstances of life, where even limited rational choice may not be an available "choice" option (e.g., Milgram, 1963); 2) It is a theory prone to blame the victim when "bad" choices are made—which is what actually happens in the selfish and cut-throat society we live in, where society doesn't take responsibility for the human beings it produces, "programs," and exhibits; 3) It does not seem to sufficiently consider the relevance of the environment or context in defining the operational parameters of the behaving individual; 4) "Power" is not, in my opinion, a basic need (as we will see in chapter seven)---I would have preferred the word *Potential* to describe the need "to be able," which is what I hope Dr. Glasser meant; and 5) *Choice theory* cannot explain all behavior in both living and non-living objects/subjects at all times. It is difficult to imagine how choice theory can explain behavior that happens in unstructured, spontaneous, or unstable circumstances.

The Explanation of Behavior: A Control Theory of Everything

I see choice theory as a tool to address reality moving forward in the process of effecting and changing beliefs in an individual who is motivated to embrace rationality. The same way Dr. Ellis used *rational-emotive* therapy to debunk the irrational beliefs of depressed clients, *choice theory* is a way of using the client's own cognitive potential to force him or her to *choose* behaviors that match the reality at hand and promote the need satisfaction of the individual.

Information Processing Theories

Information processing theories are based on the idea that all behavior and cognitive activity consists of information processing and communication more or less in the same way computers process and analyze information.

Since we live in the *information age*, these models have a strong appeal. The funny part, though, is that we humans have been around longer than computers. Therefore, if there is any similarity between computers and human beings, that is because we have been (and continue to be) attempting to model computers after ourselves, and not the other way around. Human brain processing and communication can be best understood in the context of neurolinguistics (Stemmer & Whitaker, 1998), a complex cutting-edge science that accounts for our extraordinary ability to use language and process and communicate information and data.

Information processing theories are useful in explaining the communication aspect of psychological phenomena. They apply to and rely on a wide range of disciplines and are either part of or closely associated with cognitive and systems theories. At the present time it is difficult to think of information processing without computer technology and the internet. But whether in the past or in the future, information processing will always be a part of any psychological theory.

CONCLUSION

There are, as stated earlier, many psychological theories and many combinations of theories. I have only very lightly touched a few that are popular in the U.S.A. Each theory contributes something to the understanding of human behavior, and they all have played a role more or less relevant in the historic stages of the development of psychology as a science. Yet, with all this abundance of theories, concepts, and research, psychology *lacks a comprehensive, unifying general theory,* a succinct and clear concept, which integrates all aspects of psychology into one simple and parsimonious model.

The one major problem which has prevented integration and synthesis in personality theory is, in my view, the fact that each theory tends to address one small aspect or dimension of psychology while turning a deaf ear (or a blind eye) to other aspects and dimensions, if not outright rejecting them. If psychology were an elephant, a scientist studying its nose would naturally present a different description from another psychologist describing its tail. And, in all truth, there would still be a lot of elephant to be described in between.

So, can we scientifically predict human behavior? Can we accept a general theory of psychology and behavior that integrates all the important points of existing theories and will help answer the grand question *Why do people behave the way they do when they do?* Ever since I took my first course in psychology many years ago I became convinced that there is a better way.

I propose that there are certain laws of behavior that are true all of the time. A general theory of behavior must thus be formulated on the basis of such laws. The psychologist must be able to step away from the elephant (which is difficult to do, considering that we are the elephant) and then begin to describe what can be seen, not just of the elephant, but of its surrounding world, including other elephants, flies, birds, and water holes.

<u>Chapter 2</u>

Our Place in the Universe: In Search of a Purpose

The Explanation of Behavior: A Control Theory of Everything

INTRODUCTION

You know by now that the grand question asked by psychologists is *Why do people behave (do what they do)? What makes them tick?* While physics, chemistry, and biology made great advances during the course of the twentieth century, psychology, the science that studies behavior, has achieved little more than baby steps in the grand scheme of things. Isn't that curious? We put a man on the moon and sophisticated equipment on Mars. We fought wars, tamed electricity, sent probes into space, and saved the panda. We worship the stock market, the internet, and NFL football. Magellan died to prove that the earth is round. Amelia Earhart died to prove that she could fly around it. Albert Einstein escaped Hitler and reopened the eyes of science, but he did not want to be the leader of Israel. You get up and go to work every day, rain or shine. Your kids go to school to learn about Magellan, Earhart, and Einstein. Your neighbor does not talk to you because your guest took his parking space once. Someone you know ran the marathon twice. Your great-grandfather left Europe for the New World. A man somewhere abused his own son and killed his wife. In the news, a politician you know lied to the cameras. That same night, the news was that crime rate in America was at an all time low. At the same time, it is a fact that violence is on the rise among young teenagers and pre-teens. Also, a girl died in a fire when she went back into the burning house to save her younger sister.

The Explanation of Behavior: A Control Theory of Everything

Very extraordinary indeed! People do all these things, but they don't know why they do them. What's wrong with us? We invented the atomic bomb, give a ride to a stranger, send a card to our aunt, give speeches, write books, go to college, eat, drink, have children, but we don't know why? You don't know why people do these things either, do you? Do you know why you do what you do?

The key word is motivation. What motivates you to do the things you do? Some people will say that some people will *do* certain *bad* things because *they are bad people*, and other people will *do* certain *good* things because *they are good people*, and that is the end of the story. This is a very rigid way of thinking; and for those who think this way, psychology has no business trying to figure out anything beyond that. But suppose that a *good* person does something really *bad*, how do you explain that? You can't. And it is indeed psychology's business to explain *why* people do what they do. Psychologists cannot read minds. But it is about time that psychology takes a fresh look at the alphabet the mind uses, the code that determines behavior.

It is also time that *we* focus more on and know more about our place in the Universe and our relationship with *It*. For some of you this may mean a closer dialogue with God. For others, the task may require a deeper understanding of the spiritual meaning of your life. Yet others may need to begin with a brand new set of questions, different from those you have been asking in your life thus far. For many, this closer look may simply be a smile of recognition indicating that you have been asking the *right* questions all along, even though you may have chosen to turn a deaf ear or blind eye in the direction of the answers.

PROPOSITION

Considering all these unanswered questions, any coherent attempt to formulate a general theory of behavior, a theory that will explain all behavior all the time, and that will be useful in predicting what people will do *next* must begin with a solid dosage of common sense, humbleness, openness, tolerance for criticism, and, as Einstein would probably have said, mature intuition.

The purpose of this and the preceding chapter is to set the stage for the formulation of such a theory. So, tighten your seat belts and continue enjoying the ride.

GENERAL CONSIDERATIONS

Before presenting my ideas, I want to take my hat off to all psychologists of all times who have contributed to psychology in their own way. Most people have heard of Freud, Skinner, and Maslow. But for each of these three there have been thousands of other less famous and less known psychologists, scientists, and clinicians who have been adding to the extraordinary task of understanding behavior and motivation in humans and animals. Every idea, every theory, every bit of psychological research ever done is to be acknowledged, recognized, and glorified in my understanding of behavior and motivation as I may describe it in my writings. Nothing of what I have to say here is completely new beyond the perspective, angle, and focus (to use a photographic metaphor) through which personality theory, motivation, and behavior are considered. I have therefore the benefit of peeking at the horizon standing on the shoulders of giants (if you forgive me the cliché) all of whom deserve my respect and gratitude.

PHYSICS, CHEMISTRY, AND PSYCHOLOGY: FOOTHOLDS IN THE EVASIVE LAND OF TRUTH

Remember that in Nature nothing is lost, nothing is created, but everything can be transformed. We all have learned, and kind of know, somehow, that the *truth is in the eye of the beholder*. Having said that, however, we must understand that whether we are talking about psychology or about raising chickens, there are certain **truths** that may look as evasive as sand but are indeed as solid as rock. One must be able to accept (or at least understand) those truths as prerequisites to any successful endeavor.

Before embarking on a theory-making expedition, it is very important to me, both as a human being and as psychologist, to define, very clearly, what it is that I believe has, within myself, acquired the status of solid rock truth, even if it may sometimes look like sand to you. After all, sand is made of tiny rocks. These **truisms**, which provide the basis for the ideas I am about to describe, did not pop into my head overnight. They have been carefully screened, sorted out, seasoned and pondered within my own modest mind over most of my life. The *beliefs* (remember cognitive psychology?), or **truths**, that underlie my ideas about behavior and motivation must represent a ***consensual understanding*** of our relationship with the rest of the Universe. Taking the risk of sounding excessively pragmatic and forceful, I must say that if you don't *agree* with these *truths* (my beliefs), that means I have failed to demonstrate the obvious.

These *truths* constitute the postulates of my theory of behavior and motivation and are summarized in the pages that follow.

PRINCIPLES FOR A GENERAL SYSTEMS CONTROL THEORY OF MOTIVATION AND BEHAVIOR

Principle 1: There is only One Universe.

Everything that exists, whether known to you or not, is part of the Universe. Therefore, as redundant as the statement may sound, it is important to make it clear that there is only one Universe, *obviously*.

Principle 2: The Universe is made of Matter.

The Universe is made of matter, regardless of whether or not such matter presents itself in a tangible state. Whether matter presents itself in one of its traditional states (solid, liquid, and gas), as energy, particles, quantum relationships, or as some other state, form, or conceptualization not yet discovered or envisioned, or whether it presents itself as spiritual or divine, it is still the same matter. Furthermore, all to be written in this chapter subordinates itself to the known and unknown laws and principles of physics and chemistry. In other words, psychology (motivation and behavior) must be understood in its harmony with the Universe, of which it is part.

Principle 3: *All is* Behavior.

The word *behavior* does not apply exclusively to the activity of living organisms. Atoms, humans, rocks, ants, intestines, lakes, molecules, societies, cells, volcanoes, birds, photons, livers, planets, galaxies, electrons, etc., they all behave. Anything that exists behaves as long as you conceptualize "it" as a discrete or separate *element*, *entity* or *unit* of something, which is discernible and distinct from its environment (background).

Principle 4: *Every* Behavior *requires* Three Basic Elements.

Any behavior exists within a system that contains the following basic elements: 1) an *object* or *subject*, 2) a *background* (surrounding environment), and 3) an *observer.* When the *object* has self-regulatory **and/or** self-awareness (self-consciousness) qualities, one may call it a *subject.* This very simple premise is indeed the basis of all phenomena. In other words, *a behavior is the process of an object* or *subject relating to or interacting with its respective background.* However, unless there is an *observer* to <u>observe and conceptualize</u> such process, the process will not separate itself from the continuous flow of energy, eternal and universal change and becoming—The Universe itself. Therefore, the answer to the classical metaphysical question—*If a tree crashes in a forest and there is no one there to hear it, does it make a sound?* The answer is: *No.* If there is no observer, there is no behavior. Another less esoteric, more down to earth saying, which illustrates the same point: *"What you don't know can't hurt you"* (in an emotional sense, of course).

In nature, there are no defining boundaries separating one behavior from the next, the same way that in a chain there is no defining boundary between one link and the next--there is no beginning or ending, but any link in the chain is a potential beginning or ending. For example, electrons have been "behaving" within their atomic background for an eternity. Yet only recently (in historic terms) did we *discover* the *existence* of electrons. Since we could not conceptualize them, electrons did not exist to *us*, although they have always existed in the eternal flow of the Universe.

Principle 5: "Figure-Ground" Relationships *apply to* All Behavior.

As defined in Principle 4, within a given system, and while considering "behavior," any matter, from the smallest particle to the largest mass, must be conceptualized either as an object or as a background, but it cannot be conceptualized as both at the same time. This is the place to recognize the important contribution of Gestalt psychologists like Wolfgang Köhler (1929), Max

The Explanation of Behavior: A Control Theory of Everything

Wertheimer (1938), Kurt Lewine (1939), and Kurt Koffka (1963) among others who in Germany and in the U.S.A. during the first half of the twentieth century helped popularize the relevance of *context* or *field* in the study of perception and human group dynamics. In the language of systems/communications theory, this is to say that an observer classifies his world into *categories* (backgrounds) each of which is made up of *members* (objects or object members) (Watzlawick, Weakland, & Fisch, 1974). So if you have a category named *eating*, and the members of that category are *salivating*, *chewing*, *swallowing*, *digesting*, and *metabolizing*, then you cannot say that *eating* is also a member. Eating is at a higher, more general/abstract level than salivating, chewing, swallowing, etc.

Principle 6: There are Horizontal *and* Vertical Relationships *in* Behavior.

The Universe is made of systems that relate to one another in a continuum, the same way that links relate to each other in a chain. These relationships occur both *horizontally* and *vertically*. What this means is that systems are organized hierarchically and they communicate/interact with one another both at *equivalent levels* (horizontally--as members of the same category) and/or at contiguous *lower* or *higher* levels (vertically--between categories).

Let's take the fruit fly as an example. The eyes of a fruit fly are made of cells (each cell is a system in itself, in the sense that within each cell there are object-background relationships). All the cells that make up the eye of a fruit fly are consid-

ered to exist at the same hierarchical level of functioning called *eye*. Now, let's look at the cells that
constitute the front left leg of the fruit fly. All the
cells that make up the front left leg of the fruit fly
are at the same hierarchical level called *front left
leg*. The question is, "are the eye cells and the leg
cells at the same hierarchical level?" These two
sets of cells, though individually different and belonging to different categories (one is called eye,
the other is called leg), are indeed equivalent (not
interchangeable) in their hierarchical levels within
the higher-level system called *fruit fly*.

*Following this line of reasoning, one may
say that all living cells, in all living organisms,
are hierarchically equivalent, even though they
are not necessarily interchangeable.*

Now suppose that you look at one single
cell from the leg of the fruit fly by itself (an ob-
ject/system) and you compare it with the whole
leg of the fruit fly (another object/system). The
question is: "Do the cell and the leg exist at the
same hierarchical level?" And you already know
the answer. The answer is, of course, *no*. Although
the leg cell and the whole leg behave in a contiguous relationship, the relationship is *vertical*. The
leg exists at a hierarchically higher level than the
leg cell. In fact, the leg (at the *organ* level) constitutes the background for the leg cell (at the *cellular*
level). One can therefore conclude that **an *object
system* at any given level finds *its vertical background* in one unit of its next higher hierarchical
level. The very same object system finds its horizontal background in a collection of same-level**

**object systems, which share the same vertical
background.**

This conclusion (which applies to human behavior) can be rather disturbing if one considers that contemporary human beings often ascribe more value to the infrastructure (e.g., the body, the individual) than to the superstructure of a system (e.g., society), when in reality you and I are defined by a system larger than the individual (e.g., society, culture, a belief structure, judicial systems, spirituality), from which we extract not only our identity, but also our reassurances of *control* as individuals.

Principle 7: To an **Observer,** *all* **Behavior** *exists at an* **Optimal Point** *or* **Range** *within a* **Generalization vs. Discrimination Spectrum** *(an* **Optimal Level of Contiguity** *between an* **Object/Subject** *and* **Its Background).**

Let's look at a comprehensive-systems hierarchy with four specific examples: A mountain peak named **Mount Everest**, a man named **Joe Smith**, a parrot named **Jimmy**, and a car with license plate number **SV-979** (Table 1, below).

The highest possible hierarchical level, the *Universe*, represents a macro level (shared by all that exists), and the lowest known hierarchical level, the *sub-atomic particle*, represents a micro level. From the four examples we are considering, you can conclude that when observed from our "human" point of view, the *identity of an object is lost* both at the micro- and at the macro-level. You cannot identify Joe Smith by looking through the microscope at one molecule of guanine extracted from one of his chromosomes. One molecule of guanine is always going to look the same whether it came from Joe Smith or from his parrot "Jimmy." On the other hand, if you try to locate Joe Smith looking from a distance in a tight crowd of twenty thousand people, the task may be close to impossible. It will be even more difficult if you are looking from outer space (telescopes and other devices not allowed).

So one can say that *generalization increases as one moves towards extreme hierarchical levels* and *discrimination increases as one approaches a middle or more central hierarchical level,* which is (from the relative point of view of the observer) found at *an* **optimal level of contiguity between an object and a background**. Of course what is *extreme* and what is *middle* is relative to the level from which one is making the observation. As humans, we make our observations of the world from the parameters of our own sensory receptors--our *senses* (we sometimes enhance the parameters of our senses by adding enhancing devices such as hearing aides, lenses, telescopes, etc.). So, the ideal situation to discriminate Joe Smith (the "object") from the rest of the Universe (the crowd in which he is standing--broad background) is to have him standing right in front of you (the "observer"), so that you can appreciate the wholeness of him as an object assessed by your human eyes, ears, touch, etc.

The Explanation of Behavior: A Control Theory of Everything

Four Examples of a Human Observer's Perspective Regarding Discrimination/Recognition/Identification in the Context of the Universe

Macro Level	Universe	Universe	Universe	Universe
	Cluster of Galaxies	Cluster of Galaxies	Cluster of Galaxies	Cluster of Galaxies
	Galaxy	Galaxy	Galaxy	Galaxy
	Milky Way	Milky Way	Milky Way	Milky Way
	Constellation	Constellation	Constellation	Constellation
	Solar System	Solar System	Solar System	Solar System
	Earth	Earth	Earth	Earth
	Continent	Animals	Human Society	Vehicles
	Mountain	Flock	Race	Car
	Himalayas	Parrot	Caucasian	Ford Escort
Optimal Level of Observation (highest discrimination from a human perspective)	Mount Everest	"Jimmy"	Joe Smith	SV-979
	Rocks & Snow	Bird Organs	Human Organs	Car Parts
	Layers, Formations, Etc.	Heart, Eye, Etc.	Heart, Eye, Etc.	Piston, Headlight, Etc
	Crystals	Living Cells	Living Cells	Metal Alloys
	Molecule	Molecule (e.g., Guanine)	Molecule (e.g., Guanine)	Molecule
	Atom	Atom	Atom	Atom
Micro Level	Sub-Atomic Particles	Sub-Atomic Particles	Sub-Atomic Particles	Sub-Atomic Particles

Table 1. The shaded box represents the optimal hierarchical-level for observation of the four human-scale examples in the context of the Universe (the macro level) and sub-atomic particles (micro level).

INANIMATE SYSTEMS AND SELF-REGULATING SYSTEMS

Now that I have explained the very broad context (the background) in which behavior can be understood, we are ready to do a close-up on the more concrete aspects of behavior. As always, we must begin with a series of questions. For example, if you (the *observer*) see a plastic pen (the *object*) resting on the glass top of a desk (the *background*), is that pen (or that desk, for all that matters) behaving?

Yes. The pen is behaving (and so is the desk). But how is the pen behaving?

Behavior of Non-Living Systems

The pen behaves because it is there, because it exists. Remember, all that exists behaves (it may not behave to you only if you did not know it existed). However you may of course think that it is very silly to say that a pen is behaving on the desk... But is it really silly? As we saw in the previous chapter, whether it is silly or not, all depends on who you are and on what you believe in.

So, what is really missing in the whole idea of a *behaving pen*?

I would say that what is missing so far is our *conceptualization* of a pen behaving on a desk. In other words, unless we think of the pen as a behaving object, a pen is just a pen, an eternal link in the flow of the Universe.

The Explanation of Behavior: A Control Theory of Everything

Let's ask some *why* questions. For example, *why is the pen at rest on the surface of the desk?* Since the pen exists, it has weight (mass). Since it exists in our planet, the pen is affected by a force called gravity. Gravity pulls the pen towards the center of the earth. It cannot get there because it encounters resistance posed by the surface of the desk by means of another force called cohesion (the force that keeps the particles of an object together as a single mass). Since the cohesion of the glass that makes up the surface of the desk is, at the point of contact with the pen, equal or higher than the gravity elicited by the mass of the plastic pen, the pen stays at rest for as long as that balance or equilibrium remains undisturbed--For as long as no significant change occurs in the ***environment*** supporting the situation of a pen resting on a desktop.

Note that in this book the words *environment* and *background* are interchangeable. In the example of the pen, *environment* means not only the glass desktop, but also the air around the pen, and everything else in the room that has a contiguous or potentially contiguous relationship with the pen.

A lot of things are actually happening in a simple situation involving a pen and a desktop. First of all, *why do you, the observer, know that a pen is a pen?* Well, explaining that could be a book in itself. But let's make it simple: let's say that you know it is a pen because your senses sense and you perceive it as ***different*** from its environment. You look at it and you ***know*** it is a pen, you recognize it as such. Furthermore, its apparent characteristics remain relatively constant over time.

The pen itself also has cohesion. Otherwise its shape would not remain constant. You go to the bathroom, you come back, and it still looks like a pen. If it looks like a duck, it walks like a duck, and it quacks like a duck... It could be a fake pen, couldn't it? Of course it could, but I must not tease you that far. Let's assume it is a real pen, one that writes.

So the pen is on the glass desktop, the pen and the glass each containing a force called cohesion. At the points of contact with each other (the pen and the glass) the cohesion of the glass must be equal or stronger than the weight of the pen (the gravity), *and that is the reason why the pen is there*. Otherwise either the pen or the glass top would disintegrate, and both the pen and the glass top would be pulled towards the center of the earth.

Let's suppose there is a fire on the desk while you go to the bathroom. So the fire warmed up the pen's environment significantly. You come back in the room and what do you find? You find a molten pen on the glass top. So what happened to the pen? Well what happened is that the balance or equilibrium I mentioned above was disturbed by significant temperature changes, which occurred in the environment. The rise in temperature weakened the cohesion among the particles of the pen and, for a little while, the weight of the pen was greater than its own cohesion, so gravity pulled the mass of the pen down closer to the center of the earth. Since the now liquid pen could not go past the glass top (glass is more cohesive than plastic, and the change in environmental temperature was not significant enough to change the initial condition of the glass), the pen falls off of itself and spreads itself thin on the glass, the same way a bolder rolls down the side of a mountain, so that it gets as close as possible to the center of the earth... So now you put out the fire, the temperature goes back to normal, and the cohesion of the plastic pen goes back to what it was before. The question is, *is it still a pen?* Good question. I'll let you think about that one.

I could go on and on describing how "inanimate" objects behave, even when those objects are not thought of as having self-awareness or self-regulating mechanisms. But let's find out what self-regulating systems are.

Behavior of Self-Regulating Systems

Self-regulating systems can be classified in two main categories. There are multiple ways to describe or define these two main categories. I am going to use the expressions ***self-aware*** and ***environmentally controlled*** systems. ***Self-aware systems*** are able to initiate behavior from within the system itself and the behaviors they initiate are not necessarily consistent or in accord with the behaviors that would be expected from an equivalent environmentally controlled system. Self-awareness becomes synonymous with cognition, and human beings are the perfect example to illustrate this category of system. ***Environmentally controlled systems*** may in some instances initiate behavior from within, but, even when that happens, the behaviors are driven by external (environmental) influence in ways that are rigorously predictable, pre-determined, or programmed by a higher-level system. The car you drive to work everyday is a good example. The thermostat that controls your boiler is an even better example of this category of system. Most complex living systems actually consist of a combination of these two categories of systems.

Let's go back to the example of the pen on the desk. Only instead of a pen, let's imagine that it were a fruit fly (I don't know why I insist with the fruit fly example--or perhaps it has to do with the work of biologist Thomas H. Morgan). If the pen were a fruit fly, all the same exact principles of physics and chemistry that applied to the pen would have applied to the fruit fly, but with one major difference. The fruit fly would have flown away long before it could melt (or burn)!

Immediately, two questions come to mind. *How could it fly?* And *why did it fly?* The fruit fly could fly away because, as a *system,* the fruit fly is a very amazing one. Many things can be said about the fruit fly as a system, but, to start, you can say that the fruit fly is a self-regulating system. What this means is that the fly has the ability to "measure" or "monitor" conditions in its surrounding environment and in itself and it **can initiate actions** aimed at keeping such conditions within optimal parameters. If it is too hot in the city, the fly flies to the beach. If it gets too cool at the beach, the fly comes back to the city.

Why does the fruit fly self-regulate? The answer is: **It must have a purpose.**

The Explanation of Behavior: A Control Theory of Everything

Cybernetics and the Negative Feedback Loop

Once we talk about self-regulating systems, the term Cybernetics comes to mind. Cybernetics is an interdisciplinary science articulated during the 1940's and made popular by the publication of Norbert Wiener's book *Cybernetics: Or control and communication in the animal and the machine* (1948). One great legacy of Cybernetics is the concept of **negative feedback look**, which has been applied to virtually all aspects of contemporary technology. The negative feedback loop constitutes the basic unit of cybernetic *control*. And *control*, **as I propose, is the ultimate purpose of all behavior.**

An example of a negative feedback loop is contained in the heating system of your home. We call it a thermostat, or an automatic control. The boiler in your home is either on or off. It produces heat when it is on and it does not produce heat when it is off. Let's say you like to keep your home at an average temperature of 70 degrees. Without an automatic control, you must manually switch the boiler off when the temperature gets above 70 and on when it gets below 70. Fortunately, your heating system has a thermostat that does that for you. How does it work?

In mechanical terms, the thermostat is a switch like any other switch. It has, however, some additional parts that make it automatic. These metallic parts contract when the temperature decreases and expand when the temperature rises. Physical variations within the switching mechanism are arranged so that they interrupt the electricity to the boiler when the temperature in the environment rises above 70 and re-establishes the electrical circuit when the temperature descends below 70. This is called a *negative* feedback loop because the loop is designed to *reduce* the *discrepancy* between a desired condition and an actual condition. The desired condition (e.g., 70 degrees) is called the *reference value*, which you can set to your liking. Your thermostat must also have an *input* element (sensor), such as a thermometer (or other heat sensitive metallic components as mentioned above), which serves to take the information from the environment (let's say that the input information is 65 degrees). The element in the loop called the *comparator* compares the desired condition with the actual condition. A 5 degree *discrepancy* is detected. This detected discrepancy causes the boiler to start, which *outputs* heat into the environment. So this output causes an *impact on the environment*. The boiler will continue outputting heat until the input information matches the desired- or reference-value temperature, at which time the boiler will stop. This simple dichotomous or *binary* (as more commonly called) system operates on exactly the same principle *digital* complex and sophisticated computers use. For those of you who are mathematically inclined and appreciate the wonders of engineering, I recommend that you become familiarized with the work of William L. Brogan (1991), who literally wrote the textbook on control theory.

One can say that relatively stable and successful systems such as human beings (or human society) seek and strive to maintain **homeostasis**.

The Explanation of Behavior: A Control Theory
of Everything

A homeostatic state is an optimal state of equilibrium that represents the highest common denominator in benefits and economy of resources shared by a set of interacting systems at the same or at different hierarchical levels.

    Situation Profiling. Let's consider another familiar situation. Do you remember the salivating dog? Well, you haven't heard the last of him. Imagine a situation that contains a dog and an open can of dog food. Bringing together some basic concepts of Pavlovian behaviorism (stimulus and response), and those of the negative feedback loop, such a situation can be profiled as follows:

    Subject/system: The dog (the behaving organism);

    Background: The dog food and its smell (stimulus);

    Observer: You (the scientist);

    Type of system: Self-regulating;

    Reference Value: Satisfaction/Full stomach (desired condition);

    Actual condition: Empty stomach;

    Input: Feeling of empty stomach and the smell of food;

    Comparator: The dog's nervous system (peripheral and central);

Discrepancy: Sensation of hunger;

Output: Salivation and eating (behavior or response);

Impact on Subject/System: Satiation and satisfaction;

Impact on the environment: Food and smell of food have disappeared;

Impact on the subject: Discrepancy has been eliminated (feedback received by the subject).

Behavior Analysis. From what was discussed earlier in this chapter, you can now easily appreciate that the above *situation profile* is overly simplified. We are not dealing with just one feedback loop, but many feedback loops or systems that relate horizontally and vertically at any given moment. Let's make a list of just a few behaviors that occur within the above profile:

Stomach contracting (the physical experience of hunger);
Smelling (chemical reactions within the olfactory system);
Salivating;
Looking;
Walking towards the food;
Mouthing;
Chewing;
Swallowing;

Digesting;

Metabolizing;

Defecating (related subsequent behavior).

In behavioral jargon, this breaking down of a complex behavior into its smaller units (or feedback loops, as you now would say) is called *behavior analysis* (behaviorists, by the way, would never use the term "feedback loop" associated with behavioral analysis). Notice that feedback loops follow a unique sequence towards an *ultimate goal or purpose*--**Homeostasis**. In the example above, the purpose of the sequence is to eliminate an existing discrepancy *within the subject* itself. In other instances, such as when you lower the volume of your stereo, you are eliminating a *discrepancy in the environment* (Carver & Sceier, 1982).

Who Benefits From a Discrepancy Reduction? Regardless of whether the discrepancy exists within the subject or in the environment, the ultimate "purpose," or **the *convenience*, is always relative to a system or level higher in the hierarchy**. In the case of the Pavlovian experiment, the higher system is the dog (or is it the scientist, who will derive knowledge and control from the efficacy and success of his work?). In the example of the boiler in your home, you and your family are definitely the higher-level system that benefits from the discrepancy reduction (or is it the gas company, which continues to expand its control on the market by retaining you as a satisfied captive consumer?). The questions in parenthesis may appear to be mildly sarcastic, but they are actually valid questions, truly reflective of the comprehen- siveness and infinite scope of the concepts I am attempting to define.

CONCLUSION

Since purpose exists at super-ordinate levels (at higher hierarchical levels), the Universe as a whole has an infinite tolerance for entropy (disorder and chaos). As the ultimate category, the Universe can never be violated or threatened. In the Universe nothing is ever gained or lost. In the big picture it does not really matter whether planet Earth remains in one piece or blows up into a cloud of cosmic dust. It matters only to us, at the level of being a system named **Human** and it matters to all the other self-regulating systems that coexist with us on Earth. As it is, we, living organisms, are trapped in a chaotic environment. We, living organisms, are engaged in a timeless war against the natural entropy of the Universe. Yet, paradoxically enough, that same entropy that threatens our human existence has created the "temporary" equilibrium and optimal environmental conditions (e.g., the planetary stability) that have allowed us to exist and evolve into what we are today. Sometime into the hopefully distant future when our own Milky Way and the nearby Andromeda galaxies will eventually merge into one or when the Sun and the other Milky Way stars end up being sucked into the black hole inside our own galaxy, the Universe will not flinch or cease to exist.

To us, though, for the time being (and thanks to our self-awareness), the truth remains that we are at war with chaos. We are at war with the environment (background) **on which we depend**. We must, therefore, have the ability to initiate action (behavior) to counteract or anticipate the tendency towards disorder in our contiguous background. Unlike the pen, which "happily" melts into chaos, **the fruit fly readily flies away from the burning desk in order to sustain its integrity as a self-regulating system and <u>remain in control over its relationship with its environment</u>.** When the fruit fly loses control of its interaction with its environment, it dies. **Dying means that chaos wins over order at the individual (organism) level.** Dying means the environment takes ultimate control over the living organism.

Synthesis and Control

To summarize, a fundamental truism can be extracted from the truisms presented in this chapter: *From a living organism's point of view, purpose and control reside in the unity and synthesis of its world (environment). Purpose and control reside also in the maintenance of optimal levels of subject-environment interaction. On the other hand, analysis, disintegration, and dispersion increase disorder and chaos, and, therefore, reduce control from the organism's point of view.*

Implications for Humans

As human beings, our purpose in the Universe is to master control over our interactions with our environment/background. In doing so, we have embarked in a war against chaos and in a process aimed at increasing our degrees of freedom in our chances of survival. *Behavior represents our af-*

firmation of control in the Universe. The quest for control is at the same time a purpose and a necessity. By sustaining control, a person evades the trap of chaos, for as long as the person lives. Beyond life, there is the unity of the Universe in its eternal flow of "time," "space," and "energy/matter." Beyond life, control exists at a higher hierarchical level within the Universe – the Universe itself.

As paradoxical as this may sound, keep in mind that chaos is order in a potential state, just as order is chaos in a potential state. Human beings and all other living organism species today have been able to shape our environment out of randomness and chaos (randomness and chaos only from our human perspective, not from the point of view of the Universe, where nothing is ever lost), due to our ability to initiate action. Also by being able to reproduce, humans and other living organisms, have tricked *time*, for a *while*. We stay in control as a species, but only for as long as the species does not become extinct.

We remain at risk of losing our integrity, as long as we remain attached to a location in "*space*," and as long as we actually occupy "space" and depend on "moving parts" and on external environmental elements. Like everything else, space needs to be conceptualized and perceived before it can exist. Therefore, one can, and often does, conceptualize space as an inner dimension of oneself. This allows us to bring control to a place and dimension that could never be found in the tangible, *physical* world. As we will see in future chapters, as much as control is the purpose of all behavior in the war against chaos, those who are most happy among us (by Abraham Maslow's standards) tend to be those individuals who beat space by means of finding control in the most unexpected places within themselves. God, trust, spirituality, devotion, solidarity, and the "immortality" of the soul are six examples of how human beings have managed to *deny* the war against chaos and therefore minimize the stress and the burden that would otherwise be imposed upon us by the constant acknowledgement and awareness of our precarious condition and relatively finite status in the Universe.

On "Time" and "Space"

As a final thought on this chapter, I believe that "**time**" does not exist, because it is infinite and constant, and it is unaffected by whatever happens in the Universe. I also believe that "**space**" does not exist for the same three simple reasons. We are led to believe space exists only because we conceptualize it in terms of "distances" between masses or objects. What we refer to as space is no more than complex relationships between or amongst discernible masses (matter). In the absence of these matter/energy based reference points, "space" is infinite and constant, just like a fictional story, that you can lead and expand anywhere you want to take it. **Matter/energy** is all there is. Everything else is fiction.

Now... keep in mind that I am not a trained physicist. In fact I am not a physicist at all. I am a psychologist who is made of particles (matter), therefore please take my divagations on "time" and "space" as ignorant thoughts that some real physicist may hopefully take the time to read and laugh at and (imagine that!) translate into a mathematical formula like "E=MC². " Oops... How would I explain the "C²" part of Einstein's equation, if there is no space? Doesn't the concept of speed (the "C") and acceleration (the "²") imply the concept of space? Well... Could it be that the reason why the speed of light is constant is because space is constant?

Chapter 3

Beyond Behavior and Cognition: A General Systems Control Theory of Personality and Behavior

The Explanation of Behavior: A Control Theory of Everything

INTRODUCTION

Mankind has come up with theories to explain the surrounding world. We have classified knowledge into fields like physics, chemistry, biology, and psychology, and we have elaborated on our understanding of these fields on the basis of observations, experience, and empirical research. If this process has evolved in giant leaps in branches of knowledge like physics or chemistry, where things can be objectively measured, compared, and combined, the same has not happened in psychology, because of the complex nature of its object of study--the underlying mechanisms of behavior in organisms, and the understanding of the human mind and human behavior in particular.

Everything in the Universe behaves, as we saw earlier. For example, a physicist may speak of the behavior of a falling body. Objects exert influence on other objects. Objects interact with each other in some way or another, and this happens at all levels of matter, whether the objects are planets in space or atoms in a molecule. They all behave according to certain "expectations" or laws. Contrary to the behaviors of other objects, the behaviors of living organisms at the whole-organism level are, however, rather difficult to predict consistently and reliably.

For the purpose of my argument, an organism is defined as any self-contained open and self-

The Explanation of Behavior: A Control Theory of Everything

regulating system able to extract energy from the surrounding environment by means of an active or passive interaction with it, and able to grow and somehow reproduce itself directly or indirectly. This complex, dynamic state of existence is in fact what we think of as life.

What is, then, the difference between the behavior of non-living objects and that of organisms? The difference is, as we saw with the pen and the fruit fly, an important one. Non-living objects are passive in their interaction with their environment or, if active, the activity is controlled by the environment and the object destroys itself or loses its identity in the interactive process, as in the instance of an ice cube exposed to environmental heat---melting will occur, which is an action within the cube, but such action is totally controlled by the environmental conditions, and the consequences of such behavior are the self-destruction of the ice cube as such. Non-living objects behave exclusively according to the influence of the environment upon them and their own stable and predictable characteristics. **Non-living objects do not offer subjectively variable and proportional resistance to the surrounding environment beyond the expected constant resistance inherent to the physical essence and nature of the objects in point.** For example, the so-called properties of elements (or molecules, as in the case of water) are known and established chemistry facts that do not change (at least not until scientists consensually change the paradigm we currently use to conceptualize these subjects).

The Explanation of Behavior: A Control Theory of Everything

In contrast, organisms utilize what I like to call *subjectively variable and proportional resistance* in order to achieve or maintain homeostasis. Another thing that complex organisms do is to change the reference value in the feedback loops as these loops are executed. In other words, organisms change the rules motivated by idiosyncratic projections or anticipations of control that often make sense only to the organisms themselves.

We know that the ice cube will remain an ice cube for as long as the temperature in the surrounding environment does not rise above zero degrees centigrade. Chemistry and physics study these physical essences. Given that conditions in the environment remain constant (or, if not, that they can be measured, anticipated, or even controlled), the behaviors of non-living objects can be reliably predicted. This kind of reliability is what makes us look for Comet Halley every seventy five years or so. It is also what makes us expect the sun every morning in our window. It is possible to predict with great human scale accuracy the behavior of non-living objects, just by performing mathematical calculations based on pre-established laws of the physical sciences. To illustrate this point, one may ask: How much time will object "Z" take to go from point "A" to point "B", given a specified set of contextual parameters "Y"? (Figure 1, below).

The Explanation of Behavior: A Control Theory of Everything

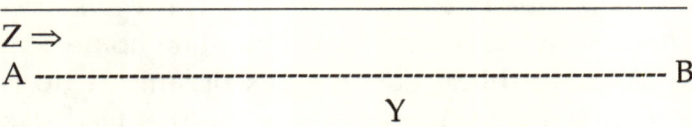

Figure 1. Illustration of Inanimate vs. Self-Regulated Objects.

If object Z remains constant in its characteristics across different trials (e.g., weight, shape, and speed), and given that points A and B remain at the same relative distance from each other and the surrounding environment Y does not change (e.g., inclination and altitude), one can be fairly certain that the time object Z takes to go from A to B will be exactly the same in every trial. Furthermore, if one changes any of the variables in the situation, one can predict the exact amount, quality, and magnitude of the impact of such change upon the other variables.

Living things enjoy all the characteristics and qualities described for non-living objects. However, because they are able to generate resistance from within (*subjectively variable and proportional resistance*), which is difficult to control for, living things interfere with the maintenance of constancy during their interactions with the environment. If one imagines that object Z was a small rock thrown in the air, one could have predicted where object Z would land (e.g., point B) and how many seconds it would take to get there. If object Z were a live bird identical to the rock in size, shape, and weight, no one could guarantee that the bird would land on point B and, if so, when.

The one main difference, then, between the behavior of non-living objects and that of living subjects is that the former can be theoretically predicted while the latter cannot **yet** be so predicted with the same scientific accuracy. Subjectively variable and proportional resistance to the environment coming from within the behaving organism is in the origin of this difficulty. As human beings, we have named this organized energy that is able to independently initiate an interaction and affect the environment (including other organisms), we have named it "soul," "mind," "drive," "life," "will," "instinct," or "spirit," just to name a few popular designations. These words indeed mean *purposeful self-organized energy* strictly in the context of my argument. Outside of my argument, these words carry significant philosophical, cultural, emotional, or religious meanings, which I want to respect. ***Purposeful self-organized energy*** is merely an addition to the list, not meant to replace any of the existing expressions outside the context of the theory I am articulating here.

PSYCHOLOGY'S SCIENTIFIC QUEST

As stated before, in order for a field of study to be regarded as science, that field has to evolve through the following developmental phases:

1. <u>Understanding</u>. The scientist must understand the parts and the whole of the object

being studied, as well as how the parts interact with each other to become the whole;

2. <u>Predicting</u>. Once a scientist understands a process or event, she or he must be able to predict its reoccurrence and outcomes;

3. <u>Controlling</u>. After having understood and successfully predicted a process or event, the scientist is then able to manipulate and control the elements or conditions involved in that process or event and guide them towards a desired outcome. In this phase, science is applied to the solution of practical problems, and we refer to it as *applied science*.

It can be deduced then that *the ultimate purpose of psychology is to understand, predict, and control behavior in animals and humans*. It is also true that this simple and innocent statement can be very controversial and can make many people upset and disappointed with my theory, because this concept can be easily confused with the idea of "external control" rejected by William Glasser (1965, 1985, & 1998). Anyone who respects freedom (and most people do, including this author) will argue that psychology is, then, attempting against the most basic rights of the organism, especially in what has to do with us, human beings.

This kind of drawback is not unique to psychology. Every science has its positive and negative aspects once it leaves the laboratory and is applied to the real world. The problem exists in physics with the application of atomic energy, in economics with the monetary system and the distribution of wealth, in genetics with cloning, and in technology in general with its great potential for comfort and pollution alike. In any of these cases science can be manipulated in favor or against the long-term survival of the organism species in question — Us!

Need for Better Communication among Psychologists

Another problem that affects the science of psychology has to do with communication among scientists. While the physical sciences are well into their *control* phase of scientific development, psychology has been struggling along in the *understanding* phase. Traditionally, psychologists continue, for the most part, to ask partial or noncomprehensive versions of the question **"Why does an organism behave the way it does?"** More than a century of serious scientific research has not been very successful in providing a unanimously accepted answer to this question. The many answers that have arisen from this diverse body of research have been too narrow and too specific. In addition, some of the available theories of behavior and personality seem unnecessarily complex and convoluted to answer the question in simple scientific terms and fall short of *explaining the purpose of all behavior*.

The lack of parsimony has added, in my view, to the already less than effective communication among psychologists working from different but not necessarily incompatible perspectives.

The Explanation of Behavior: A Control Theory of Everything

More often than not, psychologists use different theory-specific terminologies to refer to the same psychological phenomena. This may have contributed significantly to the absence of broadly accepted general laws of behavior, other than those contributed by behaviorism (e.g., conditioning), and, more recently, the neurosciences.

Manipulation of psychological elements, or factors, is not a fiction and it is not necessarily a bad thing. Psychotherapy and vocational screening are two examples of psychology venturing into its *control phase*. **In therapy the goal is to change current behavior. In vocational screening, the goal is to predict events or situational outcomes from the maintaining or enhancing of a pattern of existing behaviors, abilities, or "skills."** Successfully sometimes, and sometimes not, these ventures are not yet based on any general principle of behavior that is universally recognized and accepted. Although usually based on *a specific,* eclectic, or "multimodal" (A. A. Lazarus, 1981) theoretical approach, the outcome of these applications owes more to the clinician's intuition and experience than to scientific laws of psychology. Furthermore, I believe that most therapists and counselors, if asked the question "Why do organisms behave the way they do?" would either evade the question or answer from a specific and narrow theoretical point of view, with terminology suited not to fit other points of view (an interesting future research project). **Yet, one hundred and fifty years of psychological research has generated more than enough data that would allow us to begin working on such general laws of behavior.**

It would take only some improvement in communication among psychologists and a clear integrative direction in the work we do. Analysis is justified only if it helps in the synthesis.

Underlying Assumptions

The purpose of this chapter is to introduce a theory for the prediction of behavior based on the assumption that **any behavior, or cluster of behaviors, can be explained as an interaction between the organism and its environment**, and that an exchange of energy takes place, which follows the physical and natural laws of the Universe.

A second assumption is that **behavior is always reduced to physiological, cellular, molecular, atomic, and sub-atomic levels through a continuum** where:

1. An atom behaves in the context of other atoms (its environment);
2. A molecule behaves in the context of other molecules (its environment);
3. A cell behaves in the context of other cells (its environment);
4. An organ behaves in the context of other organs (its environment);
5. And an organism behaves in the context of other organisms (its environment).

A third assumption is that, at the organ- or organism-level, behavior is determined by the activation of specific neuron pathways in the organism. **At infra-cellular levels, behavior can also be**

determined by the direct effect of the external environment on the cells, molecules, and atoms of the organism. For instance, water, heat, or radiation can enter a cell and affect its molecules and atoms without this having been caused by neurological activity.

At these infra-cellular levels, behavior consists of chemical reactions and other physical processes (e.g., osmosis). Eventually, especially if the cells affected directly by the environment are neurons, these chemical and physical events lead to neurological activity, which may lead to organ- and organism-behavior. For example, one eats a food that creates an unusual amount of gas and pressure in the large intestine. The pressure activates the sensors that allow one to experience pain. One then heads to the bathroom or reaches for the phone and schedules a visit to the doctor.

My thesis states that **every behavior begins as a chemical reaction or as some other molecular- or sub-molecular-level physical event needed to create the electrical imbalance initiating the impulse, which then propagates throughout a neuron pathway which, in turn, acts upon other pathways, as well as muscles and other tissues (organs), causing organ- and/or organism-behaviors.**

CONTROL STRIVING: TOWARD A GENERAL THEORY OF BEHAVIOR, PERSONALITY, AND MOTIVATION

Like scientists who strive to gain control over their fields of study, organisms in general constantly strive to gain or maintain control over *selected segments* of their interactions with the environment. In fact, scientific behavior is a human example of the more general striving for control.

With some notable exceptions (e.g., Powers, 1973 & Rotter, 1989) *control* has not been a theoretical focus in personality theory, even though the concept is inseparable from psychology. A *control theory of personality* such as the one I am proposing shares many of the assumptions of other theories of behavior and personality. Most if not all existing psychological theories and research provide support, in one way or another, to the thesis I am presenting here.

Theoretical Statement

The kernel of the present thesis states the following:

Any segment of behavior at one level (e.g., at organism level) results from a cluster or sequence of behaviors taking place at lower or higher levels (e.g., organ- or society-level). Any behavior, at any level, is an attempt (not always successful) to put the organism in a position of con-

*trolling its interaction with its environment. It is,
in last instance, an attempt to keep the organism's
survival, for the organism remains alive only
while the net balance in the exchange of energy
between the organism and its environment favors
the organism. When the energy in the immediate
surrounding environment surpasses that of the organism, the organism is not able to initiate interactions or to* **resist** *against environment-initiated
interactions. When this happens, the organism as
such becomes "dead."*

Death, then, is not a simultaneous event.
The organism may stop functioning as an integrated unit, and yet most of its organs, cells, and
molecules remain intact, at least for some very
short period of time. But because the organism is
a *complex integrated system*, lack of control at one
interactive level rapidly transfers its consequences
to all other levels, both horizontally and vertically.

A basic behavior like *breathing* provides a
good example of energy exchange. The lungs exchange carbon dioxide and water vapor for incom-
ing air, which includes the *needed* oxygen. For this
exchange to take place, the organism's diaphragm
and its surrounding muscles must contract and
expand at short regular intervals, which in turn
causes the lungs to contract and expand. When
the lungs expand, the expansion increases its capacity (volume), thus lowering the inside pressure
to a level below that of the atmospheric pressure
surrounding the organism. As a result of that
sudden pressure difference, the air in the environment rushes into the lungs so that the pressure

balance can be re-established. Once the air is trapped inside the lungs, the exchange that takes place there allows the oxygen to be picked up by the circulating molecules of hemoglobin in the red cells of the blood, which in turn releases what it doesn't need (carbon dioxide and water vapor). When the diaphragm moves again, the lungs contract, thus increasing the pressure inside and expelling the "bad" air into the atmosphere, and the cycle goes on and on, for as long as the organism lives.

While the diaphragm movements in this example are genetically determined through a combined structure of neurons, muscles, skeletal, and other tissues connected to and controlled by the medulla oblongata (an area of the so called primitive brain), the air would never respond to the diaphragm activity if the atmospheric pressure were not high enough to be able to push the air into the lungs. The point to notice here is that even though both the environment and the organism play a significant role, it is the organism, and not the environment that is in control of the interaction, at least for now, while the organism is alive. The organism not only makes the diaphragm move, but also sets, changes, and adjusts its movements according to the organism's needs. If the atmospheric pressure drops, the organism breathes faster in order to maintain the same degree of control over the interaction. Death results when the organism fails to be in control of *vital interactions* such as the one just described.

Other examples of control that humans take for granted are illustrated in behaviors like *stand-*

ing, holding, walking, swimming (for those who can swim), and anything else that one can imagine doing. These behaviors usually involve movement, balance, and strength, and they usually consist of a resistance to environmental forms of energy such as gravity, temperature, and atmospheric (or other medium) conditions. Millions of years of natural selection have eliminated all individual organisms and entire species unfit to control their interaction with their environment. At any given point in time, all organisms coexisting in a given segment of environment (e.g., all living organisms on Earth right now) are the ones in control of that environmental segment--the Earth. All other organisms have become part of the non-living, they have been assimilated by the environment and have become part of the environment itself, or they have been assimilated by other organisms and thus became part of those organisms. Remember, *in Nature (in the Universe), nothing is gained or lost, but everything is transformed.*

The Role of Cognitions in a General Systems Control Theory

Not all behaviors, obviously, are as basic and easy to understand in terms of *interaction* and *control* as breathing or standing. I picked the breathing example to make my point for the same reason that geneticists choose the fruit fly to be their research subject--simple to understand and easy to observe.

In contemporary practical terms, most human behaviors arise from *representations of interactions*, not necessarily from interactions themselves. Also, for many highly complex behaviors, organisms *interpret* environmental situations instead of *sensing* them *objectively*. <u>*Organisms behave in response to what they perceive in a situation, not to what the situation actually* is</u>.

The study of **cognition** is a fascinating science in itself, and **the understanding of cognitive processes is fundamental in any attempt at predicting human behavior**, where cognitions are determining mediators. For any particular human behavior, one will be ready to understand it only after having understood its related cognitions. **It is cognitions that give the person the clue or clues as to *what it is that must be controlled* in specific interactions or in representations of interactions**. A warning sign that is written in Greek means nothing to a person who never "learned" that language. Yet, that same sign may trigger running behavior, or even a panic attack in someone who knows the language. The same stimulus elicits different strategies of control in different people, depending on a variety of conditions drawn from surrounding physical circumstances (immediate environment), experiences, values, feelings, perceptions, beliefs, attitudes, vicarious learning (Bandura, 1966) and resulting thoughts (cognitions).

Regardless of the behavior that each person will execute when in the presence of a given stimulus, <u>the purpose of the behavior is always the same</u>: To remain in control of one's interaction with the immediate environment. If you have one person who runs away from a sign that reads "DANGER! EXPLOSION IN TWO

The Explanation of Behavior: A Control Theory of Everything

MINUTES," another person who cannot read what the sign says and calmly continues to walk towards it, and yet another who also does not know what the sign says, but who cautiously walks away from it, you have three people who are doing exactly the same thing in their own unique and special way. They are exercising control over their interaction with their environment, albeit these may represent *conceptually* different levels of control. For the individual who can read the sign, the running behavior constitutes a very basic, very **_direct (vital)_** level of control. Literally, this individual is running for his or her life (or so he or she believes). For the two other individuals, who don't know what the sign says, *continuing to walk by* or *cautiously walking away from the area* constitute two examples of behaviors that are conceptualized as leading to **_indirect control_**. Indirect control is control that is not perceived as being vital to the individual "right now," but that will potentially constitute a controlling benefit to the individual at some time in the future. All play-, entertainment-, recreational-, and practice-type behaviors generate this kind of control (indirect control). Indirect control is what happens when a person goes to the opera, reads a book, plays the piano, plays golf, or engages in recreational sex (without reproductive intent). The individual experiences a feeling of wellbeing and relaxation while or after engaging in such recreational behaviors.

In the Greek-sign example above, the same situation sets different edges and levels of control for each of the three persons individually exposed

The Explanation of Behavior: A Control Theory of Everything

to it. For the one who knows Greek, control is attained if she or he evacuates self from the area in time before the "imminent" explosion. For the other two, control is attained, respectively, if 1) the peaceful walk continues without disturbance and 2) if the individual finds himself or herself walking at a "safe" distance from the mysterious sign. As we can see, true *accidents* are always the result of the organism (e.g., the person) 1) not *sensing* a stimulus, 2) having faulty, erroneous cognitions or information about a stimulus (including conflicting cognitions, which delays a response), or 3) not having the ability, the skills, or the resources (the necessary organ- or organism-level response) to perform an *escape* or proactive behavior in time to control the outcome of the otherwise disastrous interaction.

In the near future, the neurosciences will reveal with precision how cognitions are formed and processed in the brain at the cellular (neuron) and molecular levels. Interesting research has been going on for many years now involving the use of positron emission tomography (PET) scans (e.g., Nilsson, Lars-Goran & H. J. Markowitsch, 1999), to measure in real time levels of glucose consumption in specific areas of the brain as a person "thinks" and "behaves." One single thought involves the "firing" of millions of neurons both simultaneously and sequentially. One can imagine them as constellations, patterns, or clusters of neurons. For the purpose of the present thesis, I am not going to be concerned with how cognitions, units of data, or thoughts are organized in a chemical or physical sense. **I am instead going to**

focus on the *neuron pathways*, which arrive at, integrate, and depart from cognitions.

To facilitate communication, I will use words and expressions borrowed from the computer sciences and technology, since computer terminology has successfully reached the attention and understanding of a broad audience (e.g., Gates, 1996). Again, one must always keep in mind that computers are a rudimentary attempt at mimicking the functioning of the human brain. **One should never lose sight of the fact that computers are conceptually and practically subordinated to Mankind in terms of *higher control*.** Computers are better than humans in accomplishing algorithmic tasks, which is a far cry from the way our own human behavior is conceptualized and executed (and this difference is, indeed, the problem confronted by those working on artificial intelligence).

Understand and accepting a general control theory of behavior is the first step on the road to reducing human behavior to algorithmic possibilities. Nevertheless, a **perfect** or **absolute** algorithmic paradigm will never be applicable to the brains of individual humans (or other organisms), due to the fact that there are no two individuals who have identical brains and identical experiences. An algorithmic model can be applied, however, to groups of individuals, with the utilization of statistical analysis of group data and considering the margins of error acceptable in the social sciences. It can be applied to single individuals too, but only longitudinally (applying statistical analysis to patterns of behavior observed on an individual over time). In fact, these two approaches (group analysis and longitudinal single-subject designs) have been used by psychologists and by other social scientists over the years and they have been at the center of psychological applications such as law enforcement, forensic criminal investigation, terrorism prevention, and social policy development, to name a few. Nevertheless, the connection between the effort to apply an algorithmic model within a heuristics framework and a *general theory of control* is rather foreign to most people, including psychologists as a group.

Because a *pure algorithmic model* is close to impossible to be used with self-aware, self-regulating systems, *artificial intelligence* will most likely never be *like* our own *intelligence*. As human beings, we need to establish the underlying *logic* that drives our otherwise seemingly *illogical* and even *crazy* behaviors. The key rests on the mapping and predicting of the individual's *perceived locus, magnitude, and effect (consequence) of control*, not only at the linear interactive level that Julian Rotter (1966 & 1989), Bernard Weiner (1983 & 1985), and other attribution theorists have proposed (*internal* versus *external*), but, specifically, at a more **representational level** within cognitions themselves (e.g., Powers, 1973). Psychologists need to be able to measure **history**, **magnitude**, and **effect** of cognitions, not in the traditional sense of measuring cognitive functioning or *intelligence (IQ)*---which turns out to produce relatively insensitive measurements---but in terms of **beliefs**, **meaning, experience, intentionality**, and **expectations**, to name only a few relevant factors. Current psychometric efforts can be compared to the effort of a watchmaker measuring the pin of a wristwatch with a construction measuring tape. With all due respect for the beautifully packaged and commercially produced instruments put out regularly by the testing industry, the instruments and the concepts underlying the psychometric methods we use today are still outdated and insensitive, to say the least. Refinement continues to be necessary in the instruments' ability to account for individual differences in cognitively based factors, such as *history, style, attitude,* and *beliefs.* This is particularly important considering that the individual is always part of a larger system, to which he or she is subordinated. Social psychology concepts and cognitive processes must be viewed as inseparable when attempting to understand behavior (Fiske, 1995).

"Reality" vs. Representation

What I have been saying so far is that *any segment of behavior, be it scratching one's nose, running a marathon, killing for food, killing for "pleasure," playing golf, or simply standing, is always aimed at achieving control over one's interaction with the environment, although the actual effect of such control may be expected to be felt by the individual directly (immediately) or indirectly (at a later time).* Therefore, if psychologists are to be able to predict an organism's behaviors with any significant degree of accuracy, **we must know** *what it is that the organism seeks to control.* The psychologist must keep in mind that *what the individual seeks to control is*

uniquely perceived by that one individual at that one moment. In criminal investigations, detectives look at this retroactively and call it "the motive" of the crime. It is a *why* question meant to understand a behavior after it has occurred.

Reality is a very lonely, idiosyncratic, highly individualistic representation of something that may not even exist outside the representation itself! So the task of the psychologist of the future is rather grandiose. Cognitions must be conceptualized in terms of probability at a micro level, more or less in the same way that subatomic matter is conceptualized in quantum physics. Instead of subatomic particles one may use words or pictures (or other linguistic units that represent concepts and objects), preferences, default behaviors, patterns of motor activity, PET scan profiles, EEG patterns, etc., as the raw materials for this type of work. Since I am neither a mathematician nor a physicist, I will not attempt to speculate on how such probability calculations could be attained. Others with such expertise will hopefully pursue this challenge.

The Mechanisms of Behavior and Control

Because cognitions "interfere" with simple stimulus-response neuron connections, and because cognitions consist of neurological activity and *are* stimuli themselves, cognitions must be understood in the individual organism (humans in particular). A good understanding of situational cognitions will facilitate prediction of behavior.

Other behaviors, however, are **reflexive** or consist of **autonomic responses** to certain stimuli leading to highly adaptive types of control. Breathing, as we saw above, is an example in point of such *autonomic behaviors*.

When a stimulus is sensed by an organism, the *impulse pattern* is transmitted to the central nervous system by means of an *afferent pathway*, and the pattern is compared or checked against *genetically pre-established patterns of neurons* which, when matched, lead to *reflexive responses* without the mediation of cognitions. Seemingly, patterns of behavior that are frequently performed are almost as easily elicited as reflexes. Let us call this type of behavior *automatic behavior*. Though automatic, such responses or behaviors can be intercepted and affected by cognitions. Still other behaviors acquire reflexive or automatic characteristics only after having been affected by cognitions. The person running away from the warning sign would be an example of such behavior.

One thing to note is that *behaviors do not occur independently. They occur in clusters*, both simultaneously and sequentially. Going back to the warning sign example, when I said that cognitive interference changes the characteristics of the behavior, what in fact happens is that one behavior, or cluster of behaviors, is replaced by another behavior or cluster of behaviors: The person walks-looks-at-reads-*thinks*-runs, where only the running has the reflexive and automatic characteristics, accompanied, of course, by other behaviors in the cluster, such as perspiring, heart pounding, releasing of adrenaline into the blood stream, and so on. Furthermore, within the same cluster, some behaviors may be reflexive, some autonomic or automatic, and some cognitively mediated. In reality, this is most certainly always the case, because no matter what "higher" behavior an organism is performing, the vital behaviors at organ, cellular, and molecular levels continue to be performed simultaneously as **autonomic, reflexive** behaviors. It should also be noted that when a *crisis* is declared, all the different clusters of behavior, whether simultaneous or sequential, whether horizontal or vertical, they all **cooperate** towards one single super-ordinate control purpose or goal, usually at the organism level--**the purpose is to "save" the organism**. But, in some instances, such control can be focused at the species level (e.g., Humanity), or even at higher levels (e.g., Nature)! Often the locus and focus of control may be assigned to another organism perceived by the subject as part of self. One example of such a situation is the true story, in the news early in 2016, where a twelve-year old boy ran into a burning house to save his father and died (Konstantinides, 2016).

When Edward O. Wilson published his controversial book on Sociobiology (1975), the controversy was not so much on his implication that behavior can be motivated by what benefits the larger group (e.g., a bird sacrifices its own life to save the flock) but by his implication that the behavior is driven by genetic affiliation, as opposed to learned behavior (the nature vs. nurture "dilemma" once again). Sociobiology theory suggests that altruistic behavior in humans is genetically motivated. As most controversies go, there is really no need for one, since both views are correct—

the sacrifice of the part (the organ, the individual, etc.) for the stability or survival of the whole (the individual, the family, etc.) is in fact genetically established in its potential, but there is one large and most significant component that is definitely learned. Why? Because it has to do with *who* or *what* we **"perceive"** as being part of us or connected to us. And that perception is in the "software" domain at least as much as it is in the "hardware" domain, to use an informatics metaphor.

The mechanisms of behavior, from input-stimulus to achieved control, are illustrated in the diagram below, where the arrows indicate the direction of communication and the thickness of the lines indicates the strength of probability of communication (flow of energy between subject and background). The thick line indicates primary, strong, and highly probable communication and the thinner line indicates secondary, weaker, and less probable communication. Keep in mind that this is a theoretical model, not a representation of data.

What the organism senses as stimuli depends upon the particular *sensory* and *afferent-system* potential with which the organism is equipped. From the point of view of the organism itself, behavior can be *conscious* or *non-conscious*, and in either case it can be *reflexive* (with possible delayed consciousness) or *cognitively mediated*. In a reflex, the nervous impulse follows *genetically predetermined afferent and efferent pathways* of communication, whereas in a cognitively mediated behavior, after cognitive mediation the impulse can follow either a *genetically predetermined-* or a *learned (acquired)-efferent pathway*, or both.

Conscious behavior can be *voluntary, automatic*, or *autonomic*. *Non-conscious* behavior can be either *autonomic* or *automatic*, but not *voluntary*. *Voluntary behavior* leads to <u>*voluntary control*</u>. *Automatic behavior* leads to <u>*automatic control*</u>. And *autonomic behavior* leads to <u>*autonomic control*</u>. *Autonomic control* is usually <u>*direct (vital) control*</u>, but it can be <u>*indirect control*</u> as well. *Voluntary* and *autonomic control* can be either *direct* or *indirect control*.

This model is represented in Figure 2 below.

The Explanation of Behavior: A Control Theory of Everything

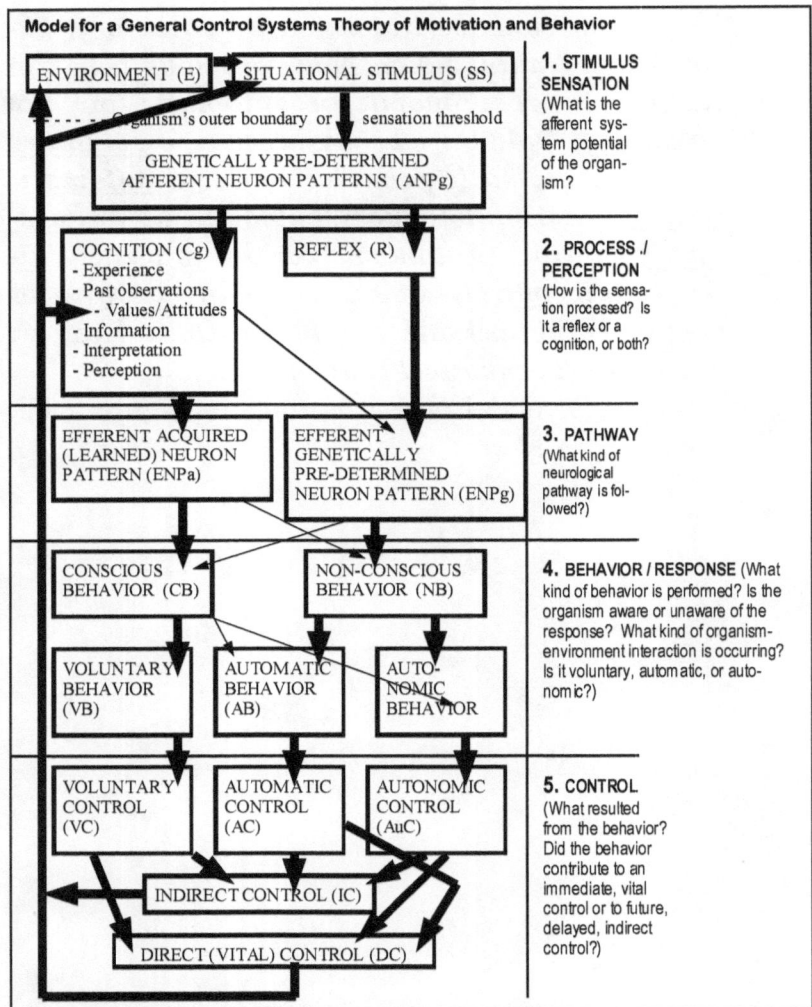

Figure 2. Model for a general control systems theory of personality and behavior.

The Explanation of Behavior: A Control Theory of Everything

Whether *direct* or *indirect*, **the degree of control attained by the organism through the behavior is fed back into the organism's nervous system and reprocessed through the same and/or different pathways. Except for some autonomic control,** an evaluative cognition of the degree of control attained in the interaction is formed and added before reprocessing. **The importance of self-assessed competence in motivation was first described in great detail by R. W. White (1959) and continues to be central to the understanding of motivation (Frankel & Ray, 1996). Cognitive self-evaluation will thus be part of the next cycle** of *sensing-behaving-controlling* **activity (the interaction) and all other cycles thereafter, until the sequential cluster is stabilized. Even after the interaction has stabilized, however, its results** (measured in *subjective, self-perceived units or degrees of control*) **will become part of the organism's experience and its cognitions, and, therefore, will have an impact on future clusters of behavior for the rest of the organism's life.**

CONCLUSION

Although the behavior of an organism is not as easy to predict as that of a falling rock, progress can be made towards prediction. Such progress can be attained if the question "Why does an organism behave the way it does?" is replaced with this other question *"What is it that (in a specific interaction with a specific segment of its environment) an organism needs or seeks to control?"* For vital types of control, behavior prediction is relatively easy to achieve because instances

The Explanation of Behavior: A Control Theory of Everything

of vital control are, for the most part, "species specific" and obvious to the observer. Considering humans as an example, one can predict with almost infallible accuracy that if a person is suddenly pushed into a swimming pool, she will initiate swimming movements soon after entering the water. One can predict the average number of heartbeats per minute in a relaxed versus anxious individual. One can predict the frequency range within which a person's voice will sound when singing versus when talking. What one cannot predict is what the person in the first example will do to whoever pushed her into the pool once she comes out. That behavior will be mediated by a complex cluster of cognitions, each with its own *feedback loop* (Carver & Sceier, 1982; Wiener, 1948) before any **hard response** (a response or behavior that can be observed by an observer) is emitted.

When cognition is involved, the person making the prediction must have available as many data as possible about the behaving subject, about the environment, and about the specific situation--its background, and history, including factors that anteceded, accompanied, and followed the interaction. In humans, the predictor (lets say, the psychologist) must know the subject's present beliefs, attitudes and values, level of education, socioeconomic status, past experiences, previous patterns of behavior, and more. For the prediction to be reliable, valid, and practical all information obtained on these factors or dimensions must be collected, organized, and analyzed statistically. Once sufficient data has been collected, psychologists will be able to predict behavior by means of consulting statistically derived tables in the same manner that IQ (intelligence quotient) scores are determined today. Of course there will be a computerized algorithm to accomplish this in fractions of a second.

If the person who pushed and the one who was pushed into the swimming pool are very close friends, and if the one who was pushed is a good swimmer and is in a good mood at the moment, and if it is a hot day, there is a strong likelihood that the person will come out of the pool with a smile on her face and friendly approach the person who pushed her, unless certain overriding or underlying predispositions will compel her to act differently. For example, if the person pushed into the pool is water phobic (in spite of her good swimming skills), or can't stand the feeling of wetness when in public, or simply cannot deal with the slightest loss of physical control, in such cases the response may be negative and unpleasant, regardless of mood, circumstances, and degree of trust and friendship.

The increasing availability of computers and computer-related technologies, including smart phones and access to large digital storage resources (e.g., Apple "I Cloud" and "Microsot Cloud"), makes it possible to store and quickly retrieve previously inconceivable amounts of information and data about individuals. When psychologists come to agree that behavior is an interaction between an organism and its environment (in actuality or in representation), and that most behaviors are mediated by cognitions, and that *all behaviors are the organism's attempt to gain or*

---

maintain control over the respective interaction, and, consequently, over its environment, then, clusters of behaviors can be studied and stored systematically. As research progresses and more data are gathered, multiple regression, correlation analysis and statistical meta-analysis of patterns of behaviors will lead psychology to the prediction of behaviors in individual organisms and in groups with a practical degree of accuracy.

In an unsystematic but promising way, we are beginning to see this type of analysis being applied in the process of identifying serial killers (often after they have killed, unfortunately). By abstracting what detectives call the "profile" or "signature" of a criminal, they can sometimes identify an individual out of a long list of possible suspects. The advertising industry and politics are other examples of this data analysis approach being used for applied purposes. We are all familiarized with surveys and polls. This technology is practically in its infancy, and such applications often develop away from mainstream psychology and in great secrecy, as they are used as instruments of *power* (refer to Chapter 7 for the distinction between power and control).

One hopes that the science of psychology will take a more central and active role not only in **reactive analysis** and modification of behavior, but also in **proactively helping** to *shape* people's behaviors from birth. Even though this deterministic and proactive approach can upset many people, as it may be perceived by some as a way to reduce the freedom of the individual, it is also true that contemporary, "civilized" societies share a common set of values that would be desirable and accepted across the board. Also, isn't it true that the process of education, with which we educate and prepare our children for the future, is indeed a predetermined curriculum that has been considered to be "good?" Most everyone would agree that a society that is cooperative, open-minded, and focused on attaining control at the level of the species as it projects itself into the future is more desirable than a society that is uncooperative, divisive, promotes violence and selfishness, and focuses on attaining control at the level of the individual.

Once we understand behavior, personality, and psychology in terms of a general systems theory of control, and once we can predict, observe, and confirm what we predict, the next logical step is to control behavior by manipulation of environmental and situational conditions.

It is reasonable to anticipate that at some time in the not distant future, the neurosciences will have developed to a point where psychologists can not only manipulate the environment as we do now, but can also artificially reprogram neurons and neuron pathways to achieve *"desirable"* behaviors in individuals. One can see how the possibility of this ever happening is controversial in itself, even though this is already happening in a rudimentary and less than scientific way. Think about this proposition the next time you get up at 5:00 A.M. and drive to work. Think about this when you see the film "Amistad" (Spielberg & Franzoni, 1997). Think about this every time you hear in the news that such and such person was sentenced to life in prison, or to die by lethal injection. Think about this every time your child or someone you know brings a reward from school or a notice of suspension. Think about this the next time you are given a speeding ticket.

Rudimentary and often ill-founded efforts to control behavior are all around us! That is part of life. Sadly, the technology of behavior modification used in homes, schools, places of work, and penal systems all over the world today has not changed much in many decades, for the most part still relying on classical and operant conditioning models. Behavior modification techniques (often misunderstood, misguided, or inappropriately applied) are the glue of society. They constitute the fabric of our social existence. There are rules for everything. If rules are broken, there is a corresponding set of consequences that applies. Individuals must do certain things in order to enhance their wellbeing or reduce pain--positive and negative reinforcement respectively. This is, nevertheless, a reactive approach to behavior modification, which does not contemplate the extraordinary sophistication of the human brain and the complexity of contemporary culture.

This commonly accepted state of affairs contains a very disturbing paradox. A child is born. Aside from his or her genetic "luggage," this child enters the world with a "clean record." This child brings into the world very specific, genetically predetermined potentials in his or her ability to succeed at interacting with the world. But *potential* by itself does not ensure success. Furthermore, we, the society, constitute this child's social environment. It seems, thus, that whether this baby will end up at the state penitentiary or at the state university will be, to a great extent, the responsibility of his or her social environment. Yet, at the society level, we are quick to point the finger and pass judgments about individuals. We like to think that individuals alone must take responsibility for their behavior (Glasser, 1998), and we seem to forget that responsibility needs to be perceived by the individual as a tool or means of control in order for the individual to be willing to engage in its exercise. How does the individual come to believe that responsibility is a good controlling mechanism? She or he needs to extract that perception from the social environment. The work of social learning psychologists is a good source of wisdom and direction when it comes to the importance of modeling and vicarious learning in society. As Albert Bandura would agree, modeling "good" behaviors for our children is the most resourceful way to ensure that they will behave "good." The "do as I say but not as I do" approach never really worked, I would think, but it works even less now, when our kids are more independent and less supervised than ever.

Because of their visibility and "power," those who embody and give a face to the structure and offices of our government should be made accountable for the responsibility of providing appropriate modeling for the citizens of the country, namely for the emerging minds of developing children and teenagers. Our political leaders should be devoted banners and untiring promoters of the values one would like to find in every community, home, or individual. If we have decided that "liberty," "justice," and "democracy" are important values in our society, how could we have overlooked **peace, tolerance**, and **accessibility to needed resources**? Isn't anyone interested in knowing why so many of our children turn out to be selfish, intolerant, aggressive, and downright criminal?

We now know that individuals are subordinated to their beliefs and expectations of themselves. Now we understand that the question is: *Do we take the time to understand why people behave and what they seek to control?* Society's institutions often show what social psychologists call "diffusion of responsibility." Educational institutions in particular, because of the nature of their role in the lives of children and young adults, must step forward not only in their mission to "educate," but also in their effort to understand where the children come from and what motivates them. We must learn to know what makes us tick before we accept and use intervention "techniques" that may do more harm than good. This is, I hope, the challenge raised in this writing.

Chapter 4

Hypothesis Testing, Theory Proving, and Data Collection: Practical and Empirical Considerations

The Explanation of Behavior: A Control Theory of Everything

INTRODUCTION

I imagine that by now you can have a different appreciation of the relationships amongst the concepts of psychology, behavior, motivation, personality, and life as it presents to you everyday. You have hopefully come to agree with me that no matter through what lenses you understand those concepts, regardless of what angle or what light you choose to apply to a situation, life boils down do **control**. As the *cliché* would best make the point, *it is all about control...* **Everything is control, and control is everything**.

Since science was invoked so much in this book, and considering that the book's content has been presented to you as a *theory*, it is only fair that you, as the reader, may want to raise questions about proving or disproving the validity of my theory and about anyone's ability to confirm or not to confirm specific hypotheses generated with the purpose of testing the theory.

This chapter is about you having fun testing my *general control theory of behavior and personality* — my *control theory of everything*.

In case I managed to confuse you in previous chapters, let me summarize my theory. It simply states that all behavior is governed by the following **seven principles**:

1. There is only one **Universe**;
2. The Universe is made of *matter/energy*;

3. All relationships/interactions (e.g., person-person, object-person, person-object, object-object) are *behavior*;

4. Every behavior requires at least **a)** an *object* or *subject*, **b)** a *background*, and **c)** an *observer*;

5. For a behavior to occur, someone or something must be able to distinguish between the object/subject and its environment/background (there must be a *perception* of that distinction);

6. There are *horizontal* and *vertical* object-background relationships in behavior;

7. All behaviors, while such, ride on the crest of an *optimal balance/equilibrium* between an object or subject and its environment or background, which allows the interaction to be perceived as a behavior in *time* (in other words, behavior is a viable process).

You must understand these principles before you are able to formulate a hypothesis on my theory. I suggest that you review them in chapter two.

Next my theory states that **all behaviors at all times** have one and **only one purpose**: *The purpose of any and all behavior at all times is for the object or subject to gain and/or sustain control over its environment.* You may always review chapters two and three to expand on this major aspect of my general control theory of behavior.

Equipped with these basic concepts, you will never again look at the world around you the same way you did before. You are now, as Dr. Harold Kelley (1967) would have said, ready to be your own scientist. You can begin designing experiments and collecting data, all in your head. You do not need a lab or a white coat. You can experiment while you wait at the doctor's office, while you drive or ride to work, or while you relax at the beach. You can experiment even while you sleep. You can experiment anytime anywhere.

GENERATING AND TESTING SIMPLE HYPOTHESES

Let's create a simple template to generate hypotheses (you can always go back to chapter one and review what I wrote earlier about hypotheses). Remember that before sticking to the hypothesis, you must design the experiment. The hypothesis is specific to the experiment. Please keep in mind that the "experiments" described below are fictional and merely illustrative.

Experiment One

Broad Question: What is the purpose of all behavior at all times?

Theory: The purpose of behavior is for an object or subject to gain and/or sustain control over its environment.

The Explanation of Behavior: A Control Theory of Everything

Narrow Question: Why do you step on the brake pedal of your car when the brake lights of the car immediately in front of you go on?

Experiment (Design): You (the subject) sit in your car and drive on the freeway at 65 miles per hour during rush hour (the environment).

Null Hypothesis: You *will not* step on the brake pedal of your car more than 50% of the time (random expectation) when the brake lights of the car immediately in front of you go on.

[Remember how the null hypothesis is stated in the negative? To make it simpler and less confusing, we will use its positive counterpart from now on].

Hypothesis: You *will* step on the brake pedal of your car more than 50% of the time when the brake lights of the car immediately in front of you go on.

Trial One Execution: Go out there, do the experiment, and record the results in terms of *YES* or *NO* responses.

Trial Two Execution: Repeat the experiment (the observation).

[Repeat the experiment as many times as you possibly can yourself and record the results. In addition, you can record the results of other drivers you observe on the road, even if they do not know you are observing them]

Results: Count the number of *YES*s and the number of *NO*s. The larger the number of trials and the more people you included in your observations (study), the more reliable the results will be and the more significant will also be any difference be between the number of *YES*s and the number of *NO*s.

Analysis of Results: Lets say that between your own trials and your observations of other drivers, you obtained a combined total of 1000 *YES*s and *NO*s, 850 of those being *YES* and the other 150 being *NO*. Statistically, your hypothesis was confirmed, because an 850 to 150 response rate cannot happen by chance. I do not want to get into statistical analysis here, as that would most likely bore you. But you know intuitively that an 85 to 15 response rate is significant when compared to the proverbial 50 to 50 null hypothesis expectation, should the **stepping on the brake** not be related to the **brake lights of the car in front of you**.

Interpretation of the Results: There has to be some reason or purpose why you step on the brake pedal more than not when the brake lights of the car in front of you go on. The reason is, according to my theory, that you, the driver, want to stay in control of that specific interaction with the environment. Taking control of that situation will preserve your personal physical integrity and that of your car, which you value, since you perceive your car as an extension of you or somehow an important part of your own existence.   There are all kinds of resources, such as money, time, and self-definition that may be directly associated with the integrity of your car, not only at the present moment, but also in the future. Therefore, *behaving* in a specific way in order to prevent an accident is not only a way of attaining immediate *direct control* (you are braking for your life) but a form of *indirect control* as well (you are making sure that you will be able to drive to work in the future, that you will not get points on your driver's license, and that you will not have expended limited financial resources on repairing a damaged car, or buying another one).

The more you consider the results, however, the more you realize that many factors came into play, especially when you attempt to explain the behavior of those people who did not step on the brake. You realize, for example, that the larger the distance between you and the car in front of you the longer it took you to step on the brake pedal of your car. You noticed that people driving bigger, sturdier, or older, neglected vehicles waited longer before stepping on the brake pedal. You noticed that you tended to push closer before stepping on the brake if you were running late to work. You also noticed that you took unusual risks, by not breaking, the day you had an argument with your husband just before you left to work. You know that these and other factors have explained the fifteen percent of the instances when the driver did not step on the brake pedal even though the brake lights of the car immediately in front went on.

Conclusion:

In conclusion, the results of your study indicated that one can predict with a fairly

The Explanation of Behavior: A Control Theory of Everything

good degree of accuracy that drivers will step on the brake pedal of the vehicle they are driving when the car immediately in front of them turns on the brake lights. They do this in order to stay in control of an environmental interaction, which could otherwise turn disastrous. In fact, your study suggests that such behavior has become *automatic behavior*, in the sense that most drivers do not have to think about it before engaging in the behavior. Yet one can also conclude that in at least 15% of the instances in which one would expect *braking behavior* to occur, individuals did not step on the brake pedal due to cognitive factors (perceptions) that mediate braking behavior in drivers. Since this study turned out to be slightly more complex than what you had possibly anticipated, there is plenty of room for future research, as you can conduct experiments or observational studies that will take into consideration some of the perception-related (cognitive) factors that may have affected the results.

For example, the actual distance between you and the car in front of you, the condition of the road at the time, the kind of car you are driving, the kind of car immediately in front of you, the type and amount of insurance coverage you have, how many times you have rear-ended or been rear-ended before, and your sense of self-efficacy as a driver, are all perception-related factors that you may consider to account for in future studies, so that you can explain the behavior of the 15% of people who did not step on the brake pedal in order to stay in control. By taking such cognitive factors into consideration you will realize that even though the behavior of *not stepping on the brake pedal* is the opposite of *stepping on the brake pedal,* the ultimate motivation and purpose of either behavior was exactly the same: To gain and/or sustain *control* over that specific interaction with the environment.

Experiment Two

Experiment one was easy, because it was an example of striving for **direct/vital control.** All such examples are easy to understand. This time let us choose something that is more like the kind of behavior not readily understood in terms of **direct control.** Most of you may have watched the now retired Larry King on television on occasion at least. I do not know him personally and I do not know more about him than you do. So to you and me he is an equally interesting subject. Let's look at one of his most observable behaviors: his routine use of suspenders.

The Explanation of Behavior: A Control Theory of Everything

Broad Question:	What is the purpose of all behavior at all times?
Theory:	The purpose of behavior is for an object, or subject, to gain and/or sustain control over its environment.
Narrow Question:	Why did Larry King choose to wear suspenders while presenting his television show?

[One obvious answer to the narrow question would be to address the functionality of the suspenders. In other words, Larry King wears suspenders with the purpose of holding his pants. But because the choice of suspenders over a common belt falls within a choice-minority in our contemporary society, one must look for cognitive mediators of control attainment]

Experiment:	Pull out six months worth of Larry King's shows and watch them at your own leisure (Larry King being the subject of your study). Count the number of shows where he is wearing suspenders.
Hypothesis:	Larry King will show up with suspenders more than 50% of the time when presenting his show.
Trial One Execution:	Watch one show and record the results in terms of *YES* or *NO*.
Trial Two Execution:	Repeat the experiment (the observation).
	[Repeat the experiment until you have watched the planned number of shows or until you get sick of watching Larry King.]
Results:	Surprise, surprise! Your hypothesis was confirmed. In fact, re-

sults may have indicated that your hypothesis was confirmed 100% of the time!

Analysis of Results: Compared with our previous study, it appears to be easier to predict whether or not Larry King will wear suspenders on any given instance of his show than whether or not people will step on the brake when the brake lights of the car immediately in front of them go on. The results of this second experiment turned out to be extraordinarily reliable. The interpretation, however, is more difficult, because the control in question is not *vital* or *direct* (except for the obvious function of the suspenders), therefore requiring a deeper cognitive analysis in search of *indirect control* yields.

The Explanation of Behavior: A Control Theory of Everything

Interpretation of the Results: Since the wearing of suspenders does not seem to be the kind of thing that stops or prevents a life-threatening situation (unless, of course, there is a health or otherwise vital reason for why he wears suspenders), one has to ascribed his rather automatic behavior (yes, non-direct behavior can establish itself as automatic behavior) to indirect control that is attained in his brain via cognitive processing (cognitions). In a true study, you would need to assess his cognitions. You would need to prepare a series of questions, methods, and strategies designed to help you understand how is it that wearing suspenders brings control to Larry King's life? It may be that somewhere somehow in his life experience, he made the association between suspenders and charismatic presence (charismatic people wear suspenders, therefore, if I wear suspenders, I am and I feel charismatic).

It may have been that one day in a rush getting ready to go to work, Larry King could not find a belt to put on and he grabbed a pair of suspenders that someone had given him two years before and he had never cared to wear. To his surprise, everybody made positive and complimentary remarks about his appearance once he got to work. The effect of this positive reinforcement on his self-esteem (remember operant conditioning?) was so strong that he developed the belief (cognition) that suspenders make him a more likeable, more respectable person. Of course, to be likeable and to be respectable are common sources of *indirect control*. To feel respected and liked by others is among the needs described by Abraham Maslow.

It may have been that Larry King walked into his studio one day, and his producer looked at him and said: "Larry... You look too plain for a man of your talent and ambitions. We are going to change your looks... Here... Put on these suspenders and shoulder pads, and we will see how the rates go." If Larry King perceived his job as having high *indirect control* value, he did as he was told and he went on with his career. Under different circumstances where insufficient or no *indirect control* value was perceived, he could have given up his job, especially if he did not like to wear suspenders.

And we could go on and on over a long list of speculations searching for the cognitive basis of indirect control in Larry King's wearing of suspenders. As you may have guessed already, the right way to do this is to ask him. People do not always understand why they do or prefer certain aspects of their behavioral repertoire, but with skill and a well-designed clinical interview, the *indirect control* value of a specific behavior will eventually surface in the context of other *indirect control* values that become thematic or recurrent. Traditional psychologists would refer to this type of effort as personality assessment. I prefer to call it **control assessment**.

The Explanation of Behavior: A Control Theory of Everything

Conclusion:

In conclusion, the results of your study indicated that specific automatic behaviors are highly predictable, even when their *indirect control value* is not immediately obvious. It also indicated that observation and reliability alone (which would suffice to a behaviorist, e.g., B. F. Skinner) does not explain the underlying cognitive processes that affected or determined the occurrence of the behavior before it became automatic. This underscores the need to obtain subjective (in relationship to the individual, Larry King in this case) cognitive material from the individual one intends to understand. As you obtain such cognitive information, you will notice patterns (e.g., beliefs and attitudes) that extend beyond the specific behavior you are trying to explain.

In addition, as you study or observe different individuals on different behaviors, you will realize that certain cognitive patterns are shared by many different individuals in the culture or society. You notice that one person's specific behavior can often be predicted or anticipated on the basis of certain family, organizational, or societal beliefs and attitudes. For example, Christian believers may process situations and ascribe meaning to stimuli arising from situations in ways that are different from those of individuals who are Jewish or Islamic believers.

The two fictional observational "studies" described above illustrate the range and scope of questions one can use to test my general control theory of behavior. I encourage you to ask specific questions and have fun confirming (or not) hypotheses. I suggest that you begin by observing and studying your own behaviors.

COLLECTING COGNITIVE DATA FROM INDIVIDUALS

Without realizing, you are collecting data from people all the time. You do it through conversation. You ask people questions. What is your name? Where do you live? What do you do for a living? How many kids do you have? We conduct these informal surveys on the go, everywhere we are. Why? Because without giving much thought to it, you need to know "where people stand on issues." It is true that the transient bus acquaintance with whom you chatted for ten minutes is not running for President, and, most likely, you will never see him again. Then, why bother asking the man where he is from and what kind of work he does? Well, because he smiled at you, and gave you the turn for you to get on the bus, he offered you the only available seat while he stood, and he remarked that he loved to see a woman dressed in yellow. Because this man triggered positive, control reassuring feelings in you, you *automatically* engaged in the process of gathering information in case you ever see him again.

But a completely different or even contrasting script could have emerged from that brief interaction on the bus. It all depends to a great extent on what you already have in your cognitive database pertaining to strangers who initiate conversation onboard public transportation. Imagine for a moment that only "bad" things resulted from

*The Explanation of Behavior: A Control Theory
of Everything*

the three previous occasions in your life when you talked to a stranger in transit. Let's also imagine that valuable and credible people in your life, from your mother and your aunt Mary to your husband John and best friends at work, they all have told you time and time again that a woman should never talk to strangers, because strangers will hurt you. In this case, you would most likely not respond to the small talk of the stranger next to you, much less ask him questions about himself. You might instead have taken a hard look at him and try to remember as many details about his appearance as you could, just in case you needed to describe him to the police.

Maximization of Control through the Acquisition of Information

In either scenario, the purpose of your behavior and cognitive processes, though literally opposed, would have been exactly the same: to maximize your control over your environment in the context of the frame of reference that applied to your beliefs about strangers. It is important to keep in mind that one's beliefs, behaviors, and cognitive processes (including one's thoughts) become so closely associated with one another (basic classical conditioning) that the relationship becomes circular and *automatic* by default. That is why beliefs are so difficult to dislodge or change once established. That is why "change" is so difficult in general when it comes to behavior, beliefs, and attitudes. The more people do something, the more likely it is they will continue doing the same.

Automatic control is often the home of crazy or irrational behavior.

The conditioning process is limited by and in fact subordinated to physiological processes that define the extent of the association between a stimulus and a response (behavior). By understanding this subordination to the physical parameters of an organism, it is easier to also understand how self-destructive behaviors such as those generally described as *addictions* are no more than automatic behaviors that no longer have control value (relative to the frame of reference of the majority of other people or to that individual at the time of occurrence), that yet continue to be executed by the individual on predictable cycles (predictable from the point of view of an observer).

For example, a young woman may try smoking for the first time in an intense and pressuring social situation where smoking gives her the impression of being liked, accepted and *at level* with her peers. This first time, and perhaps several other subsequent experiences will require effort and conscious persistence in order not to give up on the smoking effort. Positive (control value) associations will gradually be established with the act of smoking at the same time that the mechanics of inhaling smoke and physiological accommodations in the body (physical addiction) begin to gain root.

After a while, not only the young woman finds herself smoking more effortlessly and automatically, but she also finds herself smoking in situations and environments that are not the ones where she started. As the behavior became automatic, she began to generalize the positive associations and feelings initially elicited by smoking. So she may smoke at home when she is alone as a non-conscious way of feeling closer to her unavailable friends and reliving the same good feelings about herself that she experiences when in their company.

Emotions, Beliefs, and Behaviors Connection

You may have at some point in your life participated in motivation-enhancing programs or activities that required you to see, listen, think, feel and do certain things all at the same time, with the purpose of changing your beliefs and attitudes about certain aspects of your life. You may have heard of organizations that "brainwash" their members so that they (the members) can better serve the purpose of the organization. People often dance, sing, clap, run, exercise, and repeat simple easy to remember slogans, verses, riddles, or strings of words with the sole purpose of replacing one set of beliefs with another. The behavioral aspects of the conditioning process become "handles" that can be easily used and manipulated from a position external to the individual. If you are in church on Sunday morning as member of a congregation, the church ceremony follows a certain routine script designed to trigger certain feelings of religious devotion in the "hearts" of the participants. There is a sermon and readings from the scriptures; there is singing and chanting, and playing of music. There is the body language, the handshaking and the kissing.

The James-Lange Theory of Emotion

The understanding that feelings (feelings being strongly associated with beliefs) can be affected or manipulated by one's own behaviors has been around for a long time. Not without its strong critics in its time, the so-called *James-Lange theory of emotion* (James, 1890, Bernstein et al., 2000, & Schioldann, 2011) is a good example of convergent thinking on the behavior-feelings connection. If you repeatedly and persistently force your face to smile, you will surely begin to *feel* happy at some point, as it is literally impossible to sustain the incongruence of feeling sad and smiling for a long period of time. This brings to mind, of course, another landmark of psychological achievement known as *cognitive dissonance theory* (Festinger, 1957).

Cognitive Dissonance Theory

According to cognitive dissonance theory, a person's beliefs and behaviors must be consistent and aligned with each other in order for the person to experience a balanced feeling of wellbeing (I would call it a homeostatic state of *control*). For example, if you have a true strong *belief* that the Giants are far better than the Eagles, and if you have publicly declared yourself a Giants fan, your behavior while watching a match between the two teams must clearly reflect your belief and loyalty. You are expected to cheer each time the Giants score and show disappointment each time the Eagles score. By behaving in a manner consistent with your feelings and beliefs, you achieve a balanced sense of internal consonance (a sense of *control*). If the Giants lose the game, you will come up with rationalizations and explanations as to why the Eagles won, even though you believe that the Giants are the best team. The *defense mechanisms* formulated by Freud (rationalization being one of them) are all different ways of protecting consistency between *belief* and *behavior*, thus enhancing a sense of control over one's own life.

Information is important in the process of validating one's beliefs. One is constantly collecting data from the environment in order to validate one's beliefs. This data collection process leads to reassurance and indirect control. So think for a moment about what would happen to your beliefs about the Giants if the team not only lost against the Eagles today, but would also lose ten consecutive games against ten different opponents in the next several weeks? Obviously, the rationalization you used to explain away the loss against the Eagles couldn't be perpetuated to explain the ten consecutive losses that followed. You cannot say that all ten teams were lucky. At this point, the basis for a cognitive dissonance has been established. You feel very uncomfortable each time you cheer for or say great things about the Giants, simply because the facts (the information) have shaken the foundations of your beliefs about the team. Deep inside, you struggle to still *believe* that the Giants are a great team. You will struggle for as long as you cheer for them. But you will reach a point where you can no longer deal with the inconsistency. You can no longer lie to yourself. So you can only do one of two things: 1) *change the reality* of the Giants or 2) *change your beliefs* about the Giants. Since, in this hypothetical case, you cannot change the reality of the Giants, you are left with one single option: changing your beliefs about the Giants. So now, to your Monday quarterback palls' surprise, you will be bashing the Giants with the same passion you used to cheer them a few weeks earlier.

Your change in beliefs allows you now to behave *consistently* with your beliefs. You have successfully eliminated a cognitive dissonance that would otherwise drive you insane.

In fact, the more difficult it is for an individual to change his or her beliefs about something (when confronted with undeniable information or facts), the more that person will be perceived by others as odd or "strange." I can't help but to think of the two candidates running for President in the fall of 2016. The capacity of an individual to revise or change beliefs is at the basis of being able to adapt to an ever-changing environment. Extreme rigidity of the belief system can lead to less than adequate **actual control** and a higher likelihood of mental illness, unhappiness, and failure. As mentioned earlier in this book, Dr. Albert Ellis (1962) was one of the most influential psychologists in understanding the role of irrational beliefs in depression and in life in general. He developed rational-emotive therapy (RET), a form of paradoxical and confrontational cognitive therapy especially designed to dislodge even the most resistant irrational beliefs from the minds of his depressed clients.

Collecting Cognitive Data

This brings you to a simple question: *How does one then collect valid and relevant cognitive data about individuals?* The answer is disappointingly simple: *Ask them what you want to know.* Information about beliefs is the easiest to get directly from individuals, as people are often very proud of what they believe in and will not miss an opportunity to brag about their beliefs. Given neutral circumstances and in the absence of obvious negative consequences, most individuals will gladly answer your questions about their beliefs. Mental health clinicians know this fact by training, by intuition, and by observation, and that is why the art (or is it a science?) of interviewing is often at the base of any serious clinical assessment. As clinicians, we have developed the skill of shamelessly asking people the most personal, intimate, and bizarre questions that you could imagine. And we do so without blinking or smiling. A friend of mine, who is not at all familiarized with mental health (he is a mechanic) was once involved in a situation when he had to take his daughter to a psychiatrist. When I asked him the next day what he thought about the doctor, he shook his head and said, "The guy got to be retarded... He asked me a bunch of stupid questions that had nothing to do with my daughter's problem, and he kept asking me the same questions..."

Like behavior, beliefs are ever-present (in the cognitions of individuals) and like behavior, beliefs are subordinated to the purpose of maintaining an optimal level of control over the environment.

Methods of Collecting Cognitive Data

You can obtain genuine information about individuals' beliefs and thought processes in as many ways as your creativity and imagination can conceive. However, the most commonly used in research as well as in applied psychology are the *survey*, the *questionnaire*, the *interview*, the *dilemma-based essay*, the *theme-focused essay*, the *free essay*, the *interrogation*, and *naturalistic observation*. Examples of more sophisticated ways of picking people's brains on matters of belief and other cognitions are *unscripted role-playing*, *games*, *humor*, *art*, and *literature*, as well as *analyses* of their career choices, preferences in work, spouses, place of residence, activities, and leisure to name a few. A sound and reliable assessment would of course always include a combination of methods. The cognitive data one wants to extract from an individual is often found in patterns and in redundancies. Beliefs and cognitions, like behaviors, are automatic and repetitive within the person, and they can therefore be spotted and recognized in their own abundance.

Survey. Surveys can be done by phone, online, e-mail, mail, or in person. A survey consists of a set of clear and specific simple questions that can be answered with minimal effort and in a few minutes. Multiple choice or "Yes" – "No" formats are used in surveys whenever possible in order to reduce the number of variables contained in the answers and simplify the data analysis process. The survey is the method of choice to collect individual data on large numbers of people. Because surveys take only a few minutes to complete and require minimal or no personal contact with the surveyor, many people who would otherwise not submit themselves to a questionnaire, interview, or interrogation readily respond to a survey, which has become one of the most effective marketing research tools in contemporary society. Because the response to a survey is "perceived" by the respondent as a rather anonymous and inconsequent communication, people willingly provide personal and even intimate information about their preferences and choices, thus allowing a glimpse into their cognitions.

Questionnaire. A questionnaire is similar to a survey in its effort to minimize the number of variables contained in the answers, but it requires the respondent to write or speak in more detail about the question that was printed or read to him or her. A questionnaire is usually used with smaller numbers of people, as it requires more time, effort and preparation from both the questioner and the respondent. Like the survey, the questionnaire can be done by e-mail, mail, phone, online, or in person. It is the data collection instrument of choice for those engaged in serious social and psychological research. The questions in a questionnaire are more articulate and complex than those usually found in a survey. Questionnaires require more care and thoughtfulness on the part of the respondent. Many paper-and-pencil personality and other types of psychological tests are designed and meticulously crafted in questionnaire format, even though a "Yes"-"No" or multiple choice answer format may be required facilitate the standardization, reliability, and, ultimately, the validity of the results.

Interview. The interview is my favorite among all the methods used to collect cognitions from people. Clinicians like interviews because they begin with an open set of pre-determined questions that have been crafted specifically for the one individual who is going to be interviewed. As you present each question to the person, not only you get an answer to your question, but you also get a whole array of other information and clues. You have body language, mood, affect, level of enthusiasm and motivation, plus the fact that the respondent can evade or focus more or less on certain questions, or aspects of each question. But the real bonus that makes the interview a winner among the methods of collecting people's cognitions is the fact that the interviewer can skip, add, or transform any question, and follow up on any question based on the answer that the interviewee provided. Even though the data collected through interviews are not always easy to quantify, the richness and quality of the information one obtains by far compensates for any statistical inconvenience.

Dilemma-Based Essay. You can read a vignette to a person and then ask her to write an essay on how she would deal with the situation if that were to happen to her. "You went fishing in a small boat with your seventy-five year old neighbor and her seven-year old granddaughter. You are the only one who can swim. In the middle of the lake the boat unexpectedly capsizes and you all will die unless you swim to shore. There is no one around that can help, so you are all on your own. You realize that you can save one of your neighbors by swimming with only one arm, but you will not be able to save both of them. Write a two page essay on what you would do and how you would justify your choices and actions following the accident." This type of essay would provide some insight into the writer's values system in regard to children versus the elderly. It would reflect her *beliefs* about the worthiness of a child compared to the worthiness of an elderly person to say the least.

Theme-Focused Essay. The theme focused essay is similar to the dilemma-based essay, but without the dilemma. So you may ask a person to write a two-page assay on the issue of gay marriage, the war in Iraq, or stem-cell research. Make the instructions deliberately simple, open-ended, and unbiased, so that the respondent is discouraged from guessing the desirability of certain answers as compared to others. The instructions should represent a true blank canvas upon which the respondent will project his or her own preferences, choices, values, and interests.

Free Essay. With the free essay you give the person more rope so you will get more material in return. If you tell a person to write two pages on any one topic of his or her choice, you will get a genuine sample of this person's interests and choices. You may also get a flavor of the individual psychological and control dynamics, including his or her defense mechanisms.

Interrogation. Interrogation includes many of the advantages of an interview. However, the interrogation is associated with a forceful or involuntary approach to getting data and information from a person. Therefore, deception, confabulation, and stonewalling are more likely to occur during an interrogation than during an interview. Interrogations are often done in situations where there is an asymmetrical control relationship ("power" in this case, as we will see in chapter seven) between the interrogator and the respondent, who may not be allowed to leave the situation or may feel that certain responses may have more unpleasant consequences than others. A typical example of an interrogation is what happens when two-police detectives attempt to obtain information from a suspect in the process of solving a crime. Another example would be a cross examination during a court hearing, in which the respondent is a subpoenaed witness.

Naturalistic Observation. Finally, you can collect people's cognitions from observing their patterns of behavior while they go about doing the things they do everyday. As discussed above, people tend to do and to keep on doing things that are consistent with their beliefs and ways of thinking (cognitive dissonance theory). Through deduction, you may conclude that certain repeated patterns must reflect what the individual believes or thinks. If, for example, all the five brand new cars you have bought in the last twenty years are red in color, you should not be surprised to realize that your neighbors have *concluded* that you *believe* you like the color red in a car. That would be a well-established fact based just on naturalistic observation. Now, your neighbors may still be left with the question *why*. Why do you believe you like the color red? That part of the investigation would best be addressed with a simple interview, where you would be asked why you prefer the color red in the cars that you drive.

CONCLUSION

In conclusion, all organisms, including human beings, engage in the ongoing process of collecting data. Data collection is a way of obtaining crucial information about one's environment and about oneself. The more you know about your environment and about the background against which you behave the more likely it is that you will be in control of your interaction with that environment.

The emotions and beliefs of an individual are strongly connected with his or her behaviors. As such, one can change one's feelings and beliefs by changing one's behaviors, and vice-versa. The best way of assessing someone's beliefs is to ask. People are often proud to share what they genuinely believe in when asked. Other ways to assess cognitions, beliefs, and feelings are by interviewing, surveying, and observing, among other methods of cognitive data collection.

Chapter 5

The Cognitive Dynamics of Control

INTRODUCTION

In this chapter I will take you on a brief tour inside "Cognition," and together we will see why it is so true that "Perception is everything." I will also outline the three potentially different constructs of control that can be associated with one single behavior: **ideal control**, **perceived control**, and **actual control**, and how these three can differ to define an individual's level of adaptive behavior and degree of mental health, in a process I call *the cognitive dynamics of behavior*.

A TALE OF TWO ANGELS: ONE GOOD AND ONE BAD

"How can it be?" you are asking. How could an angel ever be evil? And yet the Bible tells you what happened in Paradise when Lucifer went bad and permanently damaged the outlook of happiness for the human species. If you care to remember more recent events, think of O. J Simpson, Mike Tyson, Tonya Harding, Scott Peterson, or Susan Smith. In the eyes of public opinion, a person can be good today and evil tomorrow. These shifts in the perception of behavior are always relative to some arbitrary benchmark that has been established by society or by other reference source. These sources can be a group of people (e.g., the members of an association), one person (e.g., a priest or a judge), one simple idea (e.g., the "Occupy" movement), or an entire ideology (e.g., capitalism).

The Explanation of Behavior: A Control Theory of Everything

Good Control and Bad Control

We learned early in this book that all behavior is meant to control something. But you also know, from commonsense, that some control is *good* and some control is *bad*. If you consider that control follows behavior, whether the behavior is *good* or *bad* is, in a way, a function of what kind of control is achieved or intended by the individual executing the behavior (hence the relevance of intentionality). However, the judgment on both the behavior and how control is achieved are a matter of perception in the society (social environment— e.g., public opinion, societal norms and expectations, standards, laws, and morals). In other words, the *observer* is the one who makes the ultimate determination. For example, if John enlisted in the Army, went to Iraq and killed two unarmed women, a man and a child during an encounter with the "enemy" in a Baghdad home John was not a criminal, he was a hero. John came home between deployments. He was at home with his wife and children one evening when two men broke into his house. John instinctively grabbed his pistol and shot the two unarmed assailants dead as they attempted to escape. John was now tried for charges of second-degree murder. He may be imprisoned for a long time.

Then we have the situation of a young woman, Susan Smith (Montaldo, 2015), who never had any problems with the law, had always been a good citizen, a good daughter, and a good mother until the day when she killed her two young sons and tried to blame what she did on others. She later confessed that the ***controlling*** motivation behind her actions was her ***belief*** that she would be more appealing to her lover without children than with children. It was also revealed that she had been sexually abused by her stepfather as a teenager.

As you may have already concluded, not only the same behavior can be perceived as ***good*** in one situation and ***evil*** in another, but also the same person can be perceived as being ***good*** now and ***evil*** tomorrow or vice-versa. Of course in society we tend to categorize events, things, and people as being ***good*** or ***bad*** rather than categorizing ***behaviors*** (or the ***controlling*** details associated with the behaviors). This neglect is understandable from a management of information perspective. There are so many more behaviors than there are events, things, and people (behaviors are interactions, and, therefore, there are many possible combinations), and it is easier to remember and process the latter than it is to remember and process the former. For easier assessment and management of information, it is more practical to remember that Joe, Ann, and Phil ***are*** bad and Jack, Mike, and Carol ***are*** good than to remember that all six have been ***good*** in certain specific circumstances and ***bad*** in others.

When teaching parenting skills psychologists go out of their way to tell parents never to tell children that they (the children) are bad, but to tell them instead that specific things they did (behaviors) were bad or unacceptable. By separating the ***subject*** from the ***behavior,*** psychologists hope to teach children and their parents what is acceptable and what is not without hurting their egos and self-esteem. It sounds like a very simple concept, but you would be surprised to know how many even well trained professionals (e.g., teachers, school administrators, and law-enforcement agents) refer to specific children as being "good" and to other specific children as being "bad."

Back to the Importance of Perception

Since all behaviors (good or bad) have the same purpose—to achieve some kind of control over the environment, --- it becomes obvious that *perception* in both the *subject* and the *observer(s)* determines the value (*good* or *bad*) assigned to the consequences of the behaviors. I know you must be rolling your eyes and saying "Duh! Tell me something I don't know yet." And you are absolutely right. We "all" know that. But we don't seem to think much about it and much less to practice this.

THE COGNITIVE DYNAMICS OF CONTROL

According to my theory of control, all perceptions tend to settle around a comfortable zone of consistency between the perception (cognition) and the corresponding behavior. A well-adjusted individual is one with *perceived control* (perception) that closely matches *actual control*. A person who lives for extended periods of time in constant or ongoing dissonance between perceived and actual control will display higher levels of neuroticism (e.g., anxiety) and others forms of mental illness.

The Explanation of Behavior: A Control Theory of Everything

Using the informatics metaphor once again, you may say that basic human needs are in the realm of "hardware" and "engineering," and we are very much stuck with what we got (we have a human body that needs water, food, and sleep, and can multiply itself, breath, metabolize, etc.). Perception, on the other hand, represents the "software," the add-on programs (applications) that will "make" the system produce specific "optional" results. Perceptions can be designed and programmed to fit the standards and expectations of society. For example, the language you speak, the holidays you celebrate, the laws you follow, the culture you identify with, the type of person you prefer as a mate, the foods you like, and the color of the car you like to drive (remember that one?) they all are programmed in you by society, by the environment that surrounds you. Your perception is the result of what you have learned, which means that the "good" or the "evil" you perceive as a result of the behaviors you display is all relative to what you have learned from your environment.

This last paragraph makes a profound and potentially controversial statement, because I am, to a very significant extent, taking responsibility away from the individual and placing it on the larger group (society). The *nature* vs. *nurture* debate may be easy to wind down on the account of interaction, but it cannot be put to rest considering that not all interactions *are alike*. You now know where I stand on this debate. Nature determines most of the neurological and other physical structures and parameters of the individual (his/her *hardware* potential). But learning determines most of the perceptions of control and the positive or negative value assigned to the specific behaviors that are displayed in order to achieve control.

A Model of Cognitive Control

If you refer back to the Model of General Control Theory of Personality and Behavior (chapter four), you see that with the exception of reflexive behavior, the main of all important behaviors that we display in our waken routines are filtered and processed through cognitions. As mentioned elsewhere in this book, cognitions can be conceived as being the equivalent of what behaviorists called the "black box." As an observer, you can describe the observable/measurable external stimuli that enter cognitive processing and you can observe and measure the observable/measurable behaviors that come out (responses), but you cannot really be sure of the perceptions that the subject experienced as part of that cognitive processing. In the box labeled COGNITION in the control model you can see that six arbitrary sources of contributing relevance are listed: Experience, past observations, values and attitudes, information, interpretation, and perception. I said arbitrary only because this list could include more cognitive concepts (e.g., previous learning, memory processes—attention, concentration, consolidation, retrieval---level of education, and gender). However, if you want to reduce this arbitrary list of potential contributors to one single concept, PERCEPTION is, in my opinion, the one that encompasses and represents/symbolizes the ultimate contribution to all behavior that does not stem from a reflex. As the cliché goes, "Perception is everything." And, in fact, it is. Perception will always (within your controlling dynamics) determine what you do. Perception determines your behavior.

So being (and no patronizing intended) I will take you by the hand into the box labeled COGNITION (the "black box," which can, by definition, be a very dark place). With some light from your own commonsense, intelligence, and intuition, we will look at the cognitive dynamics of control.

What is Happening Inside "Cognition?"

First, and before peeking inside the box, one must keep in mind, as the model indicates, that there are two categories of control: **Direct** (or vital) control and **indirect** (non-vital) control. This distinction, as you remember, addresses the issue of whether the control is for immediate consumption or for future use. For example, a person who chooses to eat vegetable soup today as part of a planned diet with the purpose of not developing cardiovascular disease twenty years from now is achieving indirect control over her future health. On the other hand, when the same person chooses to eat common mushrooms instead of equally available poisonous ones, he or she is making an immediate (vital) choice of control.

As you have already reasoned, most behaviors people display lead to indirect control, not direct control. Most voluntary behaviors that humans display are choice- (Glasser, 1998) or optional-behaviors of no immediate consequences for the individual's survival.

As described in chapter three, an individual's behaviors are triggered as much by external sensory stimuli as they are by the ongoing assessment and interpretations of the results of current and past behaviors. This ever-flowing cognitive feedback process is as important as the sensory stimulation and sensory perception coming in. There are, therefore, two sources of perceptual information (*sensory perception*, and *feedback perception*) and there is of course the interaction of both. They all find their home within cognition.

Let us now peek inside COGNITION. What do we see? We don't see much beyond some logical assumption about what may be going on in there, much the same way quantum physics accounts for specific subatomic particles, which cannot be observed or statically located in space. Disappointed? Don't be, as your imagination can always overcome even the most frustrating of darkness. Hold on tight to my hand.

From the observer's point of view, the assumption we visualize inside COGNITION opens a whole new dimension of control that leads to the following distinctions: *Idealized Control, Perceived Control*, and *Actual control*.

Ideal or Idealized Control. *Ideal control* is specific control that the individual would like to or hopes to achieve as the result of a specific behavior pattern. For example, a musician produces a CD (the behavior) with the intention, or at least the hope of selling 500 million copies (ideal control). You can say that *ideal control* represents the ideal consequence of a behavior, from the subject's point of view. You are speeding at fifty miles per hour in a twenty-five mile per hour zone and you hope that a police patrol will not clock you.

<u>*Perceived control*</u>. **Perceived control** is the control the subject perceives as feedback or self-evaluation once the behavior or pattern of behaviors has been executed. As you were speeding you went through the entire speed-limited zone without seeing one single police patrol car. So you perceive the results of your behavior as being successful, since the apparent consequences of your behavior matched your ideal control expectations. So you feel good, you feel lucky, you feel successful.

<u>*Actual Control*</u>. **Actual control** is the actual amount or extent of control value an individual obtains (from the point of view of an objective observer) as the real consequence of a specific behavior or cluster or pattern of behaviors. You happily drive away from the controlled-speed zone. You go home and quickly forget about the illegal behavior you executed, only to be reminded two weeks later when you receive a letter in the mail with a picture of your car's license plate and a notice indicating that you are being fined and have to go to court for speeding. Ultimately, the *actual control* for your speeding behavior was not a match either to your *ideal control* or to your *perceived control*. As you can easily conclude from this simple example, *actual control* is what effectively counts in terms of affecting your life's balance and equilibrium in your relationship with your environment. It is neither the control you

idealize, nor the control you perceive, but the control you actually achieve that makes a real difference in your life. In other words, show me the actual results of what you do, and I'll tell you how successful you are. From the individual's own subjective point of view, however, perceived control is the strongest motivator of subsequent behavior, mostly because there is very close association in time between the execution of the behavior and the perception of its impact. If you recall from classical conditioning, learning is an association between a stimulus and a response that occur close together *in space* or *in time*, or both. One's perceptions are often wrong and deceiving, thus leading to maladaptive or non-adaptive (unsuccessful) patterns of behavior.

Let's shed some light into the cognitive "black box" and see if we can figure out how these three types of control relate to each other. When we look, we find the following set o possible interactions, or, to be more politically correct, what we find is a set of possible assumptions (next page):

The Explanation of Behavior: A Control Theory of Everything

THE NINE POSSIBLE INTERACTION SEQUENCES OF CONTROL DYNAMICS					CLINICAL INTERPRETATION OF EACH CONTROL DYNAMIC SEQUENCE
1	IC*	=	PC**	=	AC***	Perfectly adjusted and mentally healthy individual (I would estimate that people who present this "jackpot" alignment all the time are difficult if not impossible to find).
2	IC	=	PC	>	AC	Internally consistent and adequately adjusted individual who tends to exaggerate the impact of his/her behavior. Overconfident individual whose level of ideal control matches his/her level of perceived control and both exceed the level of actual control
3	IC	=	PC	<	AC	Internally consistent and adequately adjusted individual who tends to underestimate the impact of his/her behavior. Low-self-confidence individual whose level of ideal control matches his/her level of perceived control, but where both ideal and perceived control fall short of his/her actual level of control.
4	IC	>	PC	=	AC	Well-adjusted highly idealistic and ambitious individual with a realistic perception of the impact of his/her behavior on the

The Explanation of Behavior: A Control Theory of Everything

						environment. This individual's level of ideal control is higher than his perceived control or actually achieved level of control.
5	IC	>	PC	>	AC	Highly idealistic individual who tends to overestimate the impact of his/her behavior on the environment.
6	IC	>	PC	<	AC	Highly idealistic and capable individual who lacks self-confidence.
7	IC	<	PC	=	AC	Pessimistic, non-idealistic individual who can make a realistic assessment of the impact of his/her behavior.
8	IC	<	PC	>	AC	Non-idealistic individual who tends to exaggerate the limited impact of his/her behaviors.
9	IC	<	PC	<	AC	Non-idealistic, low self-confidence individual who underestimates the limited effect of his/her behavior.

*IC – Idealized Control   **PC – Perceived Control   ***AC – Actual Control

Table 2. Clinical interpretation of nine possible linear control-dynamics profiles.

This table represents nine simple linear possible combinations amongst the three types of control for any given pattern of behavior. This model of interaction is based on a discrete dichotomous approach to the value of each type of control (for example, LOW versus HIGH). A continuous value option may be used, even though interpretation of data will require a more sophisticated data analysis approach.

How these three types of control dynamically play in perception is crucial to understanding adaptation of an individual in his or her interactions with the environment. To the individual in action, perceived control is what counts in relationship to that individual. Rearranging chairs on the deck of a sinking ship makes sense only to those aboard who believe (idealized control) that the ship will not sink. Looking back in History, it is easy for us (retrospective observers) to see that the way not to die on that last fatal day of the Titanic's maiden voyage was to fight for a spot in one of the lifesaving boats (actual control). The happiest, best-adjusted individuals are those with a control profile where ID=PC=AC. Of course this is an ideal profile. Most of us present close to this ideal profile most of the time. But, as the cliché goes, no one is perfect.

By the same token, one can extrapolate that mentally ill individuals or maladjusted people, as you may prefer, are persons whose control profile is IC different from PC different from AC most of the time, but of course not all the time. Even maladjusted people get it right sometimes.

CONCLUSION

In this chapter we looked at the importance of perception in an individual's dynamics of control and examined the constructs of ideal, perceived, and actual control. I went on to describe a model of cognitive control that is an integral component of the broader general control theory of personality and behavior described in this book. I also outlined the clinical interpretation of nine possible linear control dynamics sequences predicting a certain clinical profile for each sequence.

Chapter 6

The Future
of
Human Behavior

The Explanation of Behavior: A Control Theory of Everything

INTRODUCTION

In this chapter I will discuss the outlook and perspectives for the evolution of human behavior in the context of human history and the understanding of perception and control dynamics. We will look at lessons learned and will attempt to formulate possibilities and solutions for a better future. I will also discuss how theory of control relates to and interacts with religion and the concept of God.

THE FUTURE OF HUMAN BEHAVIOR

The best way to imagine the future is to study and understand the past. The future of the Universe is pretty much predictable according to the known and unknown laws of physics. We will not escape those laws for the simple reason that we have mass, occupy "space," and are attached to Earth or, in the future, to some other planet out there. For as long as we exist as subjects and observers of our own definable presence, we will ride the continuous flow of the Universe. Second to these physics (and chemistry) laws the continuation of our existence depends on our own behavior. Our so-called civilization is threatened by cosmic changes at the intra and intergalactic levels, climate changes and depletion of resources on Earth, and maladaptive behaviors within our own species.

Envisioning the future of human behavior is to predict the fate of our species.

The Explanation of Behavior: A Control Theory of Everything

How History Relates to the Future of Behavior

You may have realized that control is closely related to needs. The battles (routine control battles) that people pick stem from what they *perceive* as being relevant in their lives. The behaviors people engage in are meant to help them attain control over specific segments of their interaction with the environment that are *perceived* to be important by those individuals. Who would think of downloading music when Edison invented the gramophone, or who would care to have an automobile during the life of Marie Antoinette? Such concepts of ideal control may have existed only in the fantasies and imagination of very creative people, visionaries like Jules Verne and Leonardo Da Vinci, who described or attempted to design machinery, vehicles, and processes impossible to build or implement at the time when they were first imagined.

The more sophisticated the individual or the society where the individual lives, the more indirect and complex are the control dynamics the individual must contend with. Nomad gathering tribes have little need for elaborate and refined art consumption. They may produce or consume art only to the extent that such art is closely associated with their survival. Painting one's face and dancing to the gods so that rain will fall and berries will grow is based on deeply conditioned beliefs that are as important to their survival as the darts and arrows they sharpen in hope of a better kill.

The Explanation of Behavior: A Control Theory of Everything

As the human species becomes more dependent on knowledge and technology, it is reasonable to assume that the future of human behavior will "evolve" to serve control dynamics within knowledge and technology. I can picture you throwing your hands up in frustration saying... "But it has always been that way!" And once again you are absolutely right. The difference between now and 30,000 years ago is that now there are more things to know and more technologies to use, definitely more than what any one individual can handle. The last 150 years have been the most prolific and demanding. Especially the last 30 years have been the most transforming in terms of how exponential growth in knowledge and technology has affected our lives.

The Two Phases of Human Social Evolution

In addition to an overload of information, knowledge, and technology, another important factor that will affect the behavior of the future is the continuation of globalization and the consequent melting pot of cultures and peoples. The democratization of communications and increased physical mobility across the globe will bring the transition between two social development phases of Humanity.

**Phase one: Selfishness and Prejudice**. The first phase consists of resistance by homogeneous ethnic or national groups against the integration and acceptance of minority, "poorer," or simply "different" groups. This phase, which can last many generations, is potentially ridden with conflict, violence, and destructive feelings. During this phase, control is perceived in terms of "us against them" mentality. Since control striving always requires a subject and a background, this conflict will continue for as long as one person perceives another as being foreign, different, alien, existing outside of the self. In other words, control striving in this negative fashion will occur as long as xenophobia exists in people. This first phase is therefore long and can potentially extinguish the human species. This phase has been going on since the beginning of Humanity. The process of modern communications and integration of the world across continents began in earnest when the first Portuguese caravels left Sagres (the Bay of Lagos to be more accurate) and later Lisbon in search of new lands in the fifteenth century, but it really began to happen long before that when the first African tribes moved on to explore the surrounding lands beyond the horizon.

Think of the setbacks and injustices that Human Society has endured in these historically short six centuries of modern physical mobility around the globe! Consider slavery, the Inquisition, countless wars, the holocaust, the literal extinction of entire tribes and peoples in Africa, Asia, and the Americas, including the near obliteration of native North-Americans and their cultures through war and attrition. Think of how we, human beings, have devastated, polluted, deforested, and contaminated our planet in a few short centuries of global effort. The most recent and ongoing episode of this destructive form of globalization is taking place across the Middle East and Africa, where unresolved socio-political and nationalistic issues have brought us to the devaluation of Human life and to the complete disregard for human culture, dignity, and respect for the individual.

The bad news then is that we continue to shoot ourselves on the foot, as if we were paraplegic and could not feel that the foot belongs to us. Even a dog knows not to sleep and urinate on the same spot. We know that too. So what do we do? We eat in our own country and urinate and defecate in the country next door. Why do we do that? Because we perceive the other country as not being part of us, being something different, separate from us. We fear it if it is strong or we disrespect it if it is weak. And hence phase one of human behavior continues today. For a better understanding of what a poor job our "civilization" has done and continues to do in regards to our Human "Universality" and the distorted "Morals" we have been subjected to by our own governments, I suggest that you review the work and ideas of Noam Chomsky (Raskin, M., 2011), who has been able to denounce and articulate better than anyone else the contemporary corrupt mentality of power and exceptionality. For example, an Egyptian Air airplane went down over the Mediterranean Sea early Thursday morning on May 19, 2016. Sixty-six people reportedly lost their lives in this tragedy. And what is Bloomberg News talking about and debating, the next day, Friday, May 20? The newscast is debating how the incident may negatively affect the price of airline stocks going forward.

The good news is that because of the extraordinary communications revolution of the last few decades, individuals across the globe are able to reach out to each other faster than any government, tribe, or multinational corporations can prevent them from doing so. Individuals always do a better job at making friends than nations. As a result, we had the ideal of the Arab Spring and we have individuals dialoguing and asking questions and stimulating change all over the world. In spite of the military industrial complex, ISIS, the establishment, the new world order, the IMF, Mickey Mouse, and football, something very new and truly promising seems to be going on worldwide. Thank you, Mark Zuckerberg, for giving us "Facebook..." It is an undercurrent of human beings who see the world as a small place where we all live as one single organism. We are all horizontally connected and are part of the same thread of needs and capacities sharing the same environment we must come together to preserve. If not completely hijacked by governments the internet can be a tool--to eliminate xenophobia and promote the concept of world-citizenship, both so necessary to bring about the successful conclusion of Phase One. As Jimi Hendrix (n.d.) is credited for having said, "When the power of love overcomes the love of power, the world will know peace."

Phase two: Altruism and Cooperativism. Phase Two is a time in the future when individuals will think of themselves as citizens of the Universe. It will be a time when hunger, disease, and group-hate no longer exist. Population control will be determined by civic and moral expectations of responsibility. There will be everything of what everybody needs. Safety will be a guaranteed right. We will then live in a world of unified Humanity that will make *Walden Two* (Skinner, 1948) look like a joke. Since wars will no longer exist and Humanity will warship only one God (the Universe itself) individuals will be happy, will focus on altruistic endeavors, and will live many years, unless they die by accident, of course. Now imagine what control battles will people fight in such an ideal and utopic world! Even more importantly, will there still be a need for psychologists? Will psychologists be out of a job? Of course they will not. Rest assured that for as long as there are two people, you need a third person—the psychologist. The problems that will bring clients to psychologists will be of a different nature, though. Currently people fight and struggle to take from each other. In the future people will fight and struggle to give to each other.

Growing up without siblings close to me in age, and my sister being ten years my senior and married by the time I was nine, I always felt that I had two mothers. One thing I remember form those happy days of childhood is my sister and my mother (who lived across the street from each other) arguing on a daily basis, not about what they didn't give to each other, but about what they wanted to give to each other. Example in point, my sister (who was financially better off than my mother) would go to town and buy goodies like fresh meat, fruit, or special cookies. She would go across the street with a bag of groceries, "Here, mom, I got some extra for you." And my mother would say "No, my daughter...I don't need that," and they would argue back and forth for several minutes before my sister would finally win. My brother-in-law, who was a mechanic, would always be helping my father fixing or fabricating metallic things that broke and needed to be welded or repaired. My father, who was a mason, would, on the other hand, go and build things on my sister's property. So these were my first and most marking and enduring lessons in altruism and cooperativism. These values not only became part of who I am, but allowed me to imagine what the future of Humanity could be like. As I grew older and family of origin was no longer the main contributing factor to the development and casting of my personality, I remember feeling confused and perplexed by the realization that some siblings could actually hate each other and some parents and children couldn't get along and didn't care for each other.

Altruistic honor and recognition are concepts almost alien to our current society, guided by greed and self-interest. But in the future these will become the source of interpersonal conflict. Yes, humans will never live without conflict! Conflict is part of being alive.

Like many other things in the Universe, Phase One and Phase Two are not always mutually exclusive. On the contrary, even though at the present time most of the world seems preoccupied with war and violence, there are places on this small planet where people are ahead of their times promoting Phase Two values. One example of such an effort is the Kingdom of Bhutan, a small country squashed between India and China, where Happiness, not money, has been determined to be a measure of the nation's development and success (Grover, 2012). Instead of speaking of Gross National Product (GNP) Bhutan assesses its state of affairs in terms of Gross National Happiness (GNH).

Redefinition of Values in the Future

So, let's put all this in perspective. In the future (we don't know how soon this future will be reality if at all) people will be citizens of the Universe. They will have all their physical and material needs met and couples will not have more than two children, averaging one child per individual adult. The values of that global community will hinge on mutual respect, altruism, and the right and the obligation to live in a safe world. Well-adjusted people will be those who share the most, help the most, trust the most, and create the most. To take long naps, working from home, and having sex more than once a day will not be considered "bad" or peculiar behaviors. In fact, marriage as we know it may have disappeared or become rare. There will be no constraints on the shape and nature of the nuclear family constellation. Jealousy and love will be impossible to eradicate in the future. After all people are not perfect, remember? However, their understanding of control dynamics will help them resolve and overcome such irrational issues. Forgive me for saying that love is irrational, but it is what it is... In my own defense, I must say that I can hardly imagine a world without love. I am also certain that not everyone will think like Mr. Spock and the world of the future will definitely not look like Star Trek. In the future, control dynamics will be taught in schools across the world beginning in preschool, alongside with math, reading, geography, science, and history of the world. Other subjects taught in schools will include character development, interpersonal tolerance, and sharing economics. Capitalism, Communism, Latin, and Greek will be elective fields of study in the department of historic curiosities.

A new form of rationalism. Since emotions will be guided by thought, people will, over time, be naturally selected for bigger brains and smaller "hearts..." I am just kidding. Actually, bigger brains will require bigger hearts. Your descendents will live well into their second century of life. Two-hundred year olds will not be uncommon. Your good genes will give them a good start. But a scientifically calibrated diet, preventive medicine, gene splicing, cultured organ transplants, nano-technologies, and super medications, amongst other unknown great things to come will take care of the rest.

Most physical work will be done by thought-triggered and thought-driven robots and profit and greed will no longer rule. Keep also in mind that when in the absence of intrinsic or extrinsic motivation organisms (including humans) are economists of effort--naturally lazy. Because of this, I have some concerns about the *exercising* behavior of the future. Most likely people will lie around doing nothing—kidding again. People will play physical games as part of their exercise routines. Common people will engage in competitive sports not much different from the sports of today, but aimed at being participative and interactive. The concept of money will have become obsolete and useless---we will live in a "Moneyless World" (e.g., Shellabarger, 2006, & Ellin, 2012). The idea of having large masses of people (spectators) supporting a small elite of indulged and spoiled performers (the players and their business proxies) will not have a place in the human society of the future. People will have plenty of time on their hands and they will play and create at will.

Energy of the future. We will live in a world sustained by what we call today the alternative energies. Almost everything will run on electricity. Solar (including wind and hydraulic) and thermal energy will be literally free and abundant decentralized sources of energy reigning among all others. Energy grids will continue to exist, but merely as back up and emergency solutions. The home of the future, though connected to other homes for practical and cooperation needs (e.g., Fresco, J. & Meadows, R., 2016) will be freestanding and absolutely independent, much the same way an automobile would be today if it were self-powered, as it will be in the future, which will allow for people to live, work, and play anywhere they like.

Yet for those situations when public transportation (e.g., magnetic high speed trains) does not serve the purpose, personal transportation will be done through the air. Individuals will move around and about in capsule-like vehicles that will be designed by Apple- and Google-like organizations (which by then will not be corporations but more something like cooperatives of talent). These flying capsules, which, of course, will be called "I Move" (just pulling your leg... Who knows what these things will be called...) will come in individual, pair, and family sizes. The reason why we don't have flying cars today is not so much because of their cost or the potential pollution they would bring about (who would care about those in our current Phase One of development!), but due to the fact that the government doesn't know how to regulate what would be a very crowded and chaotic air space and avoid mid-aid collisions. However, with the current and new generations of self-monitoring devices that are already being applied in cars and can be easily programmed to create a safety bubble around any object, I anticipate that this manifestation of the future will very possibly occur in your lifetime. In fact this is already beginning with the so-called drone mania that is descending upon us.

__Democracy of the future__. Representative democracy will be a thing of the past. After all, who represents who in our current "democratic" systems throughout the world? Let's look at the United States as an example. How can Congress represent the people of this country if candidates for Congress need to have access to many millions of dollars to even consider running? Moreover, these millions of dollars are not build up of five-dollar contributions given to candidates by individuals like you and I. These millions of dollars are built from lump sum contributions by multinational corporations and the so-called super PACs (political action committees) who then uphold their purely capitalist values and keep the elected legislators hostage of their interests.

Direct democracy will prevail based on a reliable and secure super internet, which will put to shame the internet as we know it today. With the exception of a conceptual framework of operations, the government will be for the most part decentralized and virtual. Bills and law proposals will be posted daily online, by any citizen, similarly to how one would post a video on "Youtube" today. All citizens will have a moral obligation to review what is posted and vote according to their individual choices and preferences within a values system that reflects altruism, solidarity, a global vision and perception of self, and the dignity of individuals, Mankind, and Nature (Nature being simultaneously the essence and the habitat for Humanity).

Bills and law proposals will remain online for a specified amount of time to allow people to research, debate, and think of what is in the best interest of Humanity. The government will be coordinated by a new breed of webmasters — the ruling class of the future. The populous will look at this new class with some contempt, mistrust and criticism, almost the same way we think of politicians in power today. A main difference though, is that these webmasters will be nominated and elected directly by the people and will hold short six-month assignments on a voluntary basis. They will be "drafted" to serve based on their record of ability and moral and social integrity.

The Explanation of Behavior: A Control Theory of Everything

Role of the Government in the Future. The role of the government is to ensure, maintain, and coordinate the execution of a future constitution that will have been designed to reflect the technology of the future and the guaranteed entitlements of all human beings in a post-capitalism, post-greed era. The dynamics of control in this type of society will play themselves in the context of these dignifying values. Individual recognition will be then as it is today a source of self-esteem and gratification. All able individuals are expected to work (contribute to society) within their areas of expertise and interest. Work days will be very short and schedules will be flexible and variable according to need, interest, and individual choice.

Privacy of the Future. In the future everyone will be identified by biometric scanning. There is no need to carry physical identification or value objects. Every individual will be in a Universal database accessible to all. The concept of privacy will not be exercised in the realm of asset ownership of personal data as we understand it at the present. Since the only use for knowledge and information is to do-good to others, there is no point in hiding one's weaknesses or strengths. Those will be part of the public domain.

Antisocial members in this type of society will be contained, not for punishment, but for rehabilitation whenever possible or for safety when rehabilitation is not viable. This society will, to a great extent, take responsibility for the maladaptive behaviors of its members, rather than assigning the blame and responsibility solely to the individuals themselves.

A Universal Bill of Human Rights. In the future there will be a new Universal Bill of Human Rights which will provide the basis for the governing constitution. Individuals' entitlements will be in the areas of physical integrity, Human dignity, contributing to society, self-development (including education), and access to all needed resources. Since work as we think of it today will be a thing of the past, individuals will have to create and expand new and more refined ways of exercising indirect control (e.g., competition), so that they will keep their "tools" sharp and on the cutting edge of relevance. Keep in mind that we come from the caves, and it will be awfully difficult to get rid of those genes that program us to be competitive, aggressive, and anticipate struggle for survival. In fact, these very characteristics will never disappear, as we will continue to need them to survive against always emerging threats in our environment, be it new invading plants that may disrupt our food supply, mutated insects that could literally and easily outnumber and devour us, dangerous viruses, or threats from outer space, whether it may be an approaching asteroid or a hostile alien invasion.

The entire primitive brain would need to be completely overhauled if we were ever to become a docile and submissive society. That possibility seems highly unlikely and improbable considering that such a natural evolutionary process would require millions of continuous years of blissful life for humans living in a favorable and supportive environment. So my prediction is that we will always live with that potential for aggressiveness and that we will learn to reroute and "sublimate" (as Freud would have thought of it) those prewired "instincts" into ever more benign and altruistic forms of indirect control within our species and even extending such harmless control to other species of plants and animals that we consider dear to us (e.g., our pets and our backyard wild life).

In the future, indirect control will become ever more important and sophisticated, as the rules and complexity of games, sports, and other recreational activities that individuals will spend their time on will also become more complex and detailed, and, along with art and other forms of creativity, will replace labor in its almost entirety. The current money game and the business superstructures of today, like the stock market, will most certainly resist extinction, even though the concept of money is likely to evolve into a more abstract and intangible entity. Instead of a credit score, individuals will likely be viewed in light of their observable levels of altruism, trustworthiness, global cooperative attitude, self-experienced happiness, and personal history. The question of the future will not be "How many angels can dance on the head of a pin?" or "What is your credit score?" but rather "How much happiness can you bring to the Universe?" — A more personal and interactive form of religious attitude.

In the future, instead of asking a child "What would you like to do when you grow up?" we will ask the child "What would you like to control when you grow up?" This kind of question presupposes an existing awareness of control dynamics in society, which begins early in life and is part of the educational curriculum, so that even young children understand what makes people tick and the "why" of behavior. Most kids will probably answer that they want to be a "fireman," "police officer" or "football player..." I can see you squirming in your reading chair wondering if I am confused or have lost my mind—Isn't that what they say now? Well... The truth is that "Kids will be kids..." They will say they want to be the future versions of what impresses them now, with adult values that they recognize... To imagine what those activities might be is pure speculation. Hopefully these activities of choice will reflect values of a unified human society determined to live in harmony with itself and its surrounding environment. I usually follow up and ask kids why they would like to be a fireperson, or a police officer, or whatever else they have said. Young children are often sincere and honest in their answers. The most common explanation I hear from very young children about why to be a police officer is "Because I get to have a gun," or "I get to drive the police car," or "get to ride on the fire truck," for those who pick "firefighter." As kids get older, their justification is more likely to be along the lines of "I can go after the bad guys," and by mid-adolescence, I usually hear "I want to help people and keep society safe." The common denominator here is the fact that the gun and the truck are tangible transactional objects perceived to be necessary in order to assert "control," something their parents most likely believe as well.

The Explanation of Behavior: A Control Theory of Everything

From my clinical work with children, I have gotten the impression that the "gun" in particular seems to cast an impressive spell on the young child's understanding of control. I suspect that parents themselves do not purposefully set out to teach their children that to hold a gun is to have "power" and control, but that children learn this from watching violence on television, watching and playing violent videogames, and simply by interacting with other children in some communities that either talk about or have access to guns themselves. It is a sad prerogative indeed to assume that a society needs to bring its members into compliance and goodness by the barrel of a gun, so inconsistent with a species of large brains and extraordinary potential for growth, self-development, and problem solving.

In the future, we will continue to behave like human beings, but we will be very aware of our own depth and we will understand that children do what we do and not what we tell them to do or what we say we do. In other words, of all the mechanisms of learning we have reviewed in this book, social learning theory will continue to be the underlying driving force catapulting us forward to our unknown destination. Experience, cognitive mediation (e.g., perception), conditioning, and all other mechanisms of learning will always play contributing roles as well. Yet, the hope for a mature well established and applied Universal Bill of Human Rights rests mostly on our ability to model for our children and teach them--by what we say and what we do--that the righteousness of Humanity resides not in the violence of a gun, but in the tolerance, empathy, and solidarity we share in our relationships with each other. Neither the National Rifle Association (NRA) nor the United States Department of Defense, for example, would support this concept, I suppose. It is amazing how most so called developed countries do not have a Ministry or Department of Peace, Human Dignity and Wellbeing, but they do have a Ministry or Department of Defense, surely an euphemism for "Department of War" (Raskin, M., 2011) with budgets in a scale beyond the comprehension of the average citizen.

CONCLUSION

In this chapter we ventured into imagining a rather optimistic outlook for the evolution of human behavior, an attitude I owe to the memory of my professor and mentor Milton Schwebel, who always reminded me that there are more people living better in the world every day than ever before. I never questioned the validity of his assertion, even at a time, in the mid-nineteen eighties, when the daily news seemed to deny his optimism.

I proposed that the evolution of human behavior consists of two phases that will continue to overlap for some time. An initial phase still going on with vengeance (which emphasizes self-centeredness materialism, nationalism, segregation, competition, and greed), and a second phase (the seeds of which we begin to envision and seem to be supported by a contemporary take on the positive and optimistic potential of globalization and exponential development in communications

The Explanation of Behavior: A Control Theory of Everything

technologies) — which emphasizes altruism, cooperation, "happiness," Human dignity, and the wellbeing of **all** human beings. This second phase of human behavior will eventually worship the Universe Itself, which will represent the basis for all religious attitudes and will redefine our human conceptualization of God.

Human behavior will evolve towards a control-dynamics based approach to problem-solving and a new form of self-awareness based on a Universal Bill of Human Rights. This ideal Phase-Two of human behavior will lead to a life of unification, self-sufficiency, and wellbeing within our species, but will not prevent us from having to engage is conflicts, struggles, and battles with aspects of the Universe that fall outside of our own window of reference. Therefore, it may actually be a good thing that our primitive brain will continue to preserve our ability to engage in active resistance and the potential for "aggressive" behavior against the environment in order to overcome what are now unforeseen detractors and unknown enemies of a united Humanity.

Chapter 7

The Future
and
Control Dynamics

The Explanation of Behavior: A Control Theory of Everything

Introduction

If you read my book this far, you must have some reaction to what you read. I hope the theory and ideas I brought to you are presented in a way that did not antagonize, disrespect, or confuse you. The greatest challenge in writing is often not what one wants to say, but how one says it. What you read in my book is not as potentially controversial today as it was when I started writing over thirty years ago, at the time when Ronald Regan was President of the United States. If my book had come to light in those days, the least I would have unfairly been called would have been "communist" by the few people who knew me (including friends and relatives). Many important events took place in the world in the last thirty-five years that have made people everywhere less isolationist, more open-minded, and better informed. The 2013 documentary *The Unbelievers* featuring the debates and interviews of Richard Dawkins and Lawrence Krauss is an example in point of how it is possible today to confront, scrutinize, and even debunk religion and religious ideas the same way one would do so with politics, political systems, or non-religious social institutions. The fall of the Soviet Union, the papacy of John Paul II (and now Pope Francis), September 11, the Iraq War, cell phones, and the Internet are only a few of the many factors that have enhanced the chance of my theory being read today in a more tolerant and open social atmosphere than in 1986. This being said, I still hope that you reacted in some way to what I wrote so far.

CRITICAL CONSIDERATIONS

Some of my psychologist colleagues are likely to criticize or discard my theory on the basis of 1) My ideas are not "new," and 2) I am too opinionated and more concerned about my own views than about the thousands of studies that are published every year on psychological phenomena; and hey may be somewhat right on both counts. As I indicated in the first chapter, nothing is really new, but all is re-invented (the same law of conservation that applies to physics and chemistry applies to ideas and communication). It is also true that the theory I present to you in this book is a projection of my own ideas, beliefs, and "certainties." I too occupy "space" and am matter and, therefore, do not escape the laws of behavior expressed in my own theory. In other words, I am no better than you and those psychologists who will take my book apart and discount it on the basis of some "perceived" overlooking of the very rules I am trying to ascertain and promote. Theorizing about human behavior is as difficult as lifting oneself off the ground by pulling on one's own bootstraps. In spite of that, I challenge anyone to prove my theory wrong. Oops!

Of course this is another potential objection my critics will use to "invalidate" the explanation of behavior presented in this book — the traditional scientific model requires that one should be able to test a theory and prove it right or wrong by changing and manipulating the independent variables. The problem is, as pointed out in chapter 3, that when we study the behavior of living things, there is no such thing as static "independent" variables. This is definitely true for all voluntary behaviors, but, to a great extent, it is also true for automatic and even autonomic behaviors. So my theory violates the principle of consistency of results, not because the theory itself is flowed, but because the nature of the variables (both independent and dependent variables) does not conform to the consistency principle expected in the physical sciences, after which the scientific model was developed. When testing social sciences theories such as the one presented in this book, we are left to rely on statistical analysis of large numbers with commonly acceptable relatively wide margins of error (e.g., intelligence tests are normed with large standard deviations and a margin of error in the 5 to 10% range, which I imagine would not be acceptable in a chemistry or physics experiment, much less in an application such as a space rocket launching).

ETHICAL, POLITICAL, AND DEVINE CONSIDERATIONS

Take any segment of behavior and develop an experiment or observation showing that such segment of behavior *is not* aimed at controlling a corresponding segment of the surrounding relevant environment. I propose that in every instance the null hypothesis will not be confirmed. This exception to the rules of traditional theory-testing (where you would expect that different independent variables would lead to different results) occurs because of the very nature of what we are theorizing about and measuring — **Behavior**. My control theory of behavior and motivation represents an integration and synthesis framework of the understanding of behavior. My control theory is deterministic in nature. In other words, regardless of what the outcome actually is, we "*know*" that such outcome "*is*" the one the organism (e.g., human being) *has determined to bring control* to the interaction in his or her favor (even when the organism is wrong or in error from the point of view of an observer). For example, an engineer designs and builds a bridge with the **determination** that the bridge will withstand the weight of a ten-ton truck rolling on it. The engineer's determination will not change even if the bridge collapses when the first five-ton truck passes over it. A determination implies intention of results, but it cannot guarantee the results.

Deterministic actions and processes are appreciated and cherished as the soul of engineering applications (most bridges do not actually fall and they do exactly what the engineer **had determined** them to do), but **deterministic proposals or ideas** often clash with and raise controversy when applied to our current western society values set of presumed individual "freedom" and "democracy," except of course in religion, where **determinism** is ok, because it comes from the "Creator" or from some other "Higher" power.

God is often referred to as an entity in *Itself*, an agent of creation *Who* created the Universe. In fact, God is often described as "The Creator." To a believer, *Only God can give or take a life.* If a tragedy strikes and an innocent child dies, a believer will say that God has *determined* there is a *reason* why this child was killed.

In this book, I make the point that the Universe created itself, and, therefore, The Universe *is* God, and all in *It* is an integral part of God. Hence, if half million men, women, and children died during the Iraq war, those people are part of God, the same way that a part of God dies when you swat a mosquito and kill it. Deepak Chopra, in his consciousness-related book, *The Future of God* (2014), expresses this definition of the Universe as God far more eloquently than I could ever do here. He makes reference to God the Creator as "God 101," good for childhood consumption, but not for a highly sophisticated self-conscious adult.

You and I are well aware of ongoing ethical controversies in areas like genetic *engineering* or social *engineering*. The word *engineering* is what usually raises eyebrows, but the real issue is the implied **determinism** contained in the word *engineering*, or, in simpler terms, the idea of "playing God." It is ok if we play God to make an internal combustion engine run, to place a man on the moon and a satellite into space, to shoot and destroy something or someone that is 6,190 miles away with the push of a button, or to make a few multinational corporations "successful" (too big to fail), but it is not ok **to *determine* our destiny as a species based on a sound understanding of Control Dynamics and its application to a decent planned future for Humanity**. Interesting indeed... Perhaps you can help me explain that. Also, I suggest you become familiarized with the visionary ideas of Jack Fresco (1994; Fresco & Meadows, 2016), a unique self-made futurist genius from whom we may learn a thing or two about how to plan and understand the future.

THE INTENTIONALITY FACTOR

Intentionality, genetically rooted in the individual's consciousness and self-awareness (the self-preservation "instinct" at its most basic level), alters the expectation of constancy that you would find in a hard sciences experiment. Because in humans intentionality is, to a great extent, a cognitive process, it will always affect the results of the experiment in a number of ways, including, for example, the purposeful display of a response (behavior) that will contradict the expectation.

Elsewhere in this book I give you the example of stepping-on-the-brake-pedal behavior while driving on the highway, when the brake lights of the vehicle just in front of you turn on. My theory predicts that you will step on the brake of the vehicle you are driving as a response to the brake lights of the other vehicle, *presuming* of course that your main goal is to prevent a hurtful accident. However, my theory also predicts that if you, the driver, are aware of the study or of the fact that you are being watched for that particular behavior, you may in fact *intentionally* not brake when you would be expected to. You might for example swerve off the road into the shoulder, to avoid rear-ending the car in front of you, or you might simply rear-end the other car, just to make your point of confirming my null hypothesis, thus "defeating" my theory.

Intentionality is applied proactively by the **subject** as a mediator of control through the subject's own behavior. But it applies as well to an observer and observer/subject's perception of others' behaviors. We are constantly "attributing" the cause of events we witness to factors that may or may not be perceived to be part of ourselves. The study of intentionality in psychology is best articulated in "attribution theory" and "locus of control" research, an area of social psychology that caught the interest and attention of some great psychologists like Fritz Heider, Harold Kelley, and Julian Rotter in the 1950's and 1960's (e.g., Heider, F., 1957; Kelley, H., 1964; Rotter, J., 1989) which is worth revisiting.

CONTROL VS. POWER

Finally, I want to clarify the very important difference between *control* and *power*. Control results from any (all) effort (behavior) we invest towards achieving an optimal level of homeostasis in our relationship with our immediate environment. Control underscores any behavior that leads to the experience of success and wellbeing of the behaving organism **with the *minimum investment of energy and minimum impact on the environment*.** Control does not require any excess in the duration, magnitude, or intensity of the behavior beyond what is necessary. Power, on the other hand, exists when the organism sustains a segment of behavior or cluster of behaviors beyond what would be necessary to establish and maintain homeostasis. Like control, theses excesses can be measured in the duration, magnitude, and/or intensity of the behavior as well as in the impact of the behavior on the corresponding segment of the environment. Power is, in other words, any behavior in excess of what is necessary for achieving **adequate** control. So, by logical deduction, and as Mr. Spock would look at it, while all power requires control, adequate control does not require power. Under this consideration, the "on" and "off" button on your home appliances should not be labeled "power" but "energy control" instead. The fact is that in the English language, the words "power" and "energy" have come to acquire the same meaning in some applications. This is true also for the common association of the word "control" with the concept of "negative manipulation," when "control" is indeed a neutral word that merely defines the expectation of what follows behavior.

For example, let's say you are a police officer walking down the street. You get to a point where three men are talking on the sidewalk blocking you from passing. If your behavior is *"Excuse me, gentlemen, let me pass through..."* you are exercising control. If, instead, your behavior is to *pull out your gun and wave it in the air* to scare the three men away you are exercising power. We sometimes refer to people who engage in "abuse of power." By its own definition, power is always abusive. **Power and abuse are the same**. They always represent an excess of some behavior, which results in the expenditure of energy beyond what is required to achieve control and have a homeostatic and harmonious impact on the immediate environment. Much more needs to be written about power and control, but for now we may leave them at that. As food for thought, one may say, for example, that in many instances **control is or can be** *power* **in a** *potential* **state**.

One myth that needs to be debunked about control (as I define control in this theory of behavior, motivation, and personality) is the idea that control is tangible. In fact, the most effective and efficient forms of control are not physical or manipulative in nature. **Control dynamics** amongst people, for example (and as defined in chapter 5), do not refer to negative forms of tangible control often associated with the word. The word "control" without a context is almost by default erroneously associated with some kind of interpersonal, social, physical, or psychological repression, coercion, or negative manipulation. It is true that such repression, coercion, and manipulation do exist (as you and I unfortunately so well know based on our experiences with abusive individuals who have crossed our paths), but in reality they are merely one approach to attain control and represent a minute percentage of an infinite number of far more intangible and harmonious approaches.

To say that control is "bad," because some people use power (excessive control) to reach their self-perceived goals and attain their self-perceived needs would be the same as saying that water is "bad" because floods occasionally occur and kill people, or that behavior management is "bad" because some people and institutions use punishment instead of positive and negative reinforcement. Behavior management is bad only when punishment is the approach of choice to achieve the goal or when the intended goal is to *intentionally* "hurt," mislead, or otherwise affect others against their own self-interests. Control is "bad" only when power is used as the approach to achieve the goal. In other words, and to make it simple, **control** cannot be bad, unless it is "**power.**"

This distinction between **control** and **power** is relevant not just pertaining to individuals, but to institutions, societies, and nations. For example, slavery was an institution of power. Even though it was practiced by individuals (the slave owners), the institution of slavery was pretty much an accepted and legitimate component of society until relatively recently. Though more covertly and often disguised as employment, slavery still exists today almost everywhere among us. Prisons, schools, multinational corporations, military and paramilitary agencies, and governments at all levels still operate today under our very own noses as institutions of power (abusive institutions) and not institutions of **control** (effective, efficient, and supportive). To our dismay, revenge and punishment are still acceptable concepts in law enforcement, jurisprudence, and schools today as deterrents or disciplinary intervention frameworks.

CONTROL DYNAMICS IN EDUCATION

Imagine an institution of education, such as a school system, vested by society with the highly honorable function of educating children. The stated goal of the system is to "educate" its students. This school system has a curriculum that has been determined to represent the basic knowledge and concepts necessary to form a responsible, independent, productive, and participating citizen.

Presumably, the educational curriculum contains a selection of codes perceived by society to be indispensable and a must learn in order for the individual to **control** his or her way through life and participate in the political process and in the shared vision of that society. By extrapolation, what one learns in school is indeed crucially important to form not only the "values" of the developing individual but also the building blocks and parameters of his or her Control Dynamics approach to life. Typically, the basic codes taught in schools are the light spectrum (colors), shapes (basic geometry), and abstract codes (representations) like a writing code (e.g., the Latin alphabet or Braille) and a numeric code (e.g., the Hindu-Arabic numerals).

Of course, as we move up in the educational process, we learn other codes such as computer programming languages (e.g., BASIC, FORTRAN, C+, Dart, Java, or Swift), and, more importantly, we learn to use the basic codes in ever more complex applications to solve problems (attain **Control**) that make us successful. For example, we

The Explanation of Behavior: A Control Theory of Everything

learn English, Spanish or German from a single or slightly modified alphabet, we understand algebra, trigonometry, and calculus using numerals, shapes, and a few operational symbols, and we design, access, and use the internet by transforming, integrating, and controlling many otherwise basic codes into the marvel we call "the digital world."

Another code we learn in school (or should learn in school) is **the code of "good manners"** and the **code of social and interpersonal ethics**. I know that this learning begins at home (or should begin at home) from day one in the child's life. But unlike the Hindu-Arabic numerals, the Greek alphabet, or FORTRAN, the code of social and interpersonal relations is subjective, often difficult to agree on and many times used as a source of **power** by those who can. It is true that in preschool and kindergarten we teach children to say "please," wait their turn, and say "thank you" once they attain the control they seek. We also try to identify and label some basic feelings for them, like "happy," "scared," and "angry."

Most kindergarteners I have met over the years in schools and through family and friends, including my own children and grandchildren, were pretty good at mastering the simple expectations of social interaction. Yet, for a great number of children and young adolescents, especially those who grow up and go to school in neglected areas of large cities, something seems to go amiss during the elementary school years. In high school, where I have worked as a school psychologist for thirteen years, teachers tell you on a daily basis that many of their students, both male and female, are rude, uncaring, disrespectful, and unmotivated to learn. I see this as well, and wonder what components of the social code we are not teaching them before they get to high school. In fairness, I should also say that the majority of high school students I have interacted with seem to know how to behave and relate to others. It is not uncommon that a small percentage of each class accounts for the sense of inefficacy and frustration expressed by teachers. When I meet the parents of these students, I usually find a correlation between the behavior of the student and the demeanor and attitude of the parent.

So, let's review this. Most kindergarteners are resourceful and active bundles of energy who not only learn the colors, the letters, and the numbers, but also how to smile, say "please" and "thank you." This flash of happiness seems to disappear, however, between first and eighth grade, when I believe the educational system should focus more on positive experiences, and character and social skills development and less on formal academic learning and group "achievement" test scores.

It is obvious that educating a child requires coordinated teamwork involving the parents, the teachers, the community, and the school leaders, who set the tone for teachers and students. Punishment, repression, authoritarianism, rigidity, fact shoving, revenge, and other forms of explicit power have no place in a school. Students must learn to trust themselves, believe in themselves, and in their future. Modeling how to adequately attain control is a fundamental feature of school leadership.

While still in college, I found myself astounded by the research findings on learned helplessness published by Martin Seligman and W. R. Miller (1975). They had shown that dogs and humans, in spite of the huge difference in cognitive abilities between the two species, could be affected by repeated inescapable exposure to pain and negative, failure experiences. Organisms learn to give up and not care if they perceive that they have no control over the interactions they have with their environment or with the outcomes of such interactions. What we tell children and what we "make" them feel, in school or at home, will surely have an impact on what they come to believe about themselves.

Elementary- and middle-school age children who feel they have no control over the outcome of their school routine, or their lives in general, are likely to give up on learning and find refuge in addictive, self-stimulating, and often self destructive behaviors, such as playing video-games, eating, calling negative attention to themselves by misbehaving, withdrawing from social interaction, or bullying others. The association of learned-helplessness and depression is true to adults as much as it is to children. Furthermore, as we discussed earlier when reviewing social learning theory, kids learn as much through their own experiences as they learn by watching what happens to their peers. Children as young as three-, four-, and five-years of age set their level of self-confidence, goal-setting, and self -efficacy based on what they learn from watching the experiences of other children their age (Guerreiro, 1989).

I owe my interest in control theory at least in part to Seligman and Miller's work. And yet, so many years later, here we are still allowing our children to find school boring and uninteresting and blaming them for failing.

While the buzz about the universal design for learning (UDL) model has, during the last fifteen years or so (e.g., Meyer & Rose, 2014), raised hopes for a better integration and support of special needs and other idiosyncratic learners in our schools, the increasingly sustained and organized attack from state governments on large city public school systems (along with some federal policy that supports privatization or semi-privatization of schools) has, instead, significantly reduced and denied students needed resources that would facilitate and support multisensory/multimodal learning in general education classrooms.

What we see is a reduction or dislocation of state funding in education budgets and large numbers of needy students with limited support at best. In my view, this state of affairs may lead to the downfall of what was, for many generations of young men and women, the great equalizer in American society—The community based and supported public school system.

Control Dynamics in Educational Curricula

In the future, I envision a school curriculum based on an ecological understanding of life that begins before conception and during pregnancy. I am presenting below an outline of what I believe is an example of a better curriculum, which the future will hopefully bring to us.

I. Every pregnant mother and her companion (when available) will attend and participate in a parenting skills training program (not re-active punishment for negligence or abuse--as government child protection services address the issue today,--but a preventative measure instead, consisting of a hands on review of what they have learned in high school about parenting). Parents to be will learn (review):

A. Control dynamics theory and its everyday practice;
B. Important facts about child development;
C. Child safe environments;
D. Healthy nutrition;
E. Healthy and safe parenting activities;
F. Child behavior management;
G. Fundamentals of character and character development;
H. Life-long planning.

II. During the **first two years of life (2 years)**, the mother will be afforded any support necessary to make sure that she will be the child's primary caregiver. The mother and/or the father will participate in parenting network groups involved in social and parenting activities while the primary caregiver will be on leave of absence from work.

III.   During ages **three through five (3 years)**, the child will attend preschool in the same building where the mother or father works. The caring parent will interact with his or her child throughout the workday during lunch and breaks. Community daycare centers similar to those in existence today would be an alternative option, where an available relative (e.g., grandpa or grandma) would be checking in throughout the day, or even volunteering at the school. The child will learn to share and play cooperatively with other children. Child will learn age-appropriate concepts following Piaget's theory of cognitive and emotional development (Wadsworth, 1996), always through fun play and high interest activities. During these three years, the child will be introduced to the fundamentals of Control Dynamics and will establish the base for sound character- and social-development. The child will learn the meaning and the importance of the following words and concepts:

A. Cooperation;
B. Sharing;
C. Tolerance;
D. Empathy;
E. Goal setting;
F. Creativity;
G. Sustained effort;
H. Helping;
I. Listening;
J. Communicating;
K. Global geography and global positioning;
L. Limited earth resources (saving and recycling);
M. Physical education.

During these very important three years, the child will also be introduced to the management of negative feelings such as jealousy, selfishness, competitiveness, frustration, depression, and anxiety. The child will be read to on a regular basis both at the daycare and at home and will watch uplifting movies and stories that illustrate the words and concepts listed above. Characters like Winnie the Pooh, Tiger, and Bugs Bunny will be in high demand (you must be smiling and thinking I am ancient... Ok... You pick your own nice contemporary characters… Oh, yeah… and Fred Rogers). During these three years at daycare, the child will also be exposed to multiple forms of visual, performing, and musical arts by watching and being given the opportunity to interact and play without any pressure whatsoever to perform. The child will be exposed to numbers, letters, shapes and colors as three-dimensional play objects. The child will be encouraged to always be cooperative but also to be creative and unique in his or her play. During these three years, children will be taught to respect Nature, Life, and The Universe. The Universe being all there is — known and unknown.

IV. Ages **six through ten (5 years)** children will receive elementary education. They will learn about:
A. Control Dynamics;
B. Reading and Writing (multiple languages);
C. Mathematics;
D. Global geography;
E. Computer programming;
F. Character development and citizenship;
G. World and Human History;
H. Science;
I. Feelings management;

J. The arts;

K. Physical education;

L. Life planning.

V. Ages **eleven through thirteen (3 years**)--middle school--the educational focus will be on:

A. Control Dynamics;

B. Character development and citizenship;

C. Life planning (including parenting);

D. Managing authority, cooperation, democracy, and public service;

E. Building consensus in decision-making;

F. Management and distribution of limited resources;

G. Time management and definition of career, occupational and vocational interests;

H. Exposure to human productive activities

    i. Invited speakers;

    ii. Work place visits;

    iii. Internships;

    iv. Apprenticeships;

    v. Teleconferencing;

    vi. Local, national, and international travelling.

I. Computer programming;

J. Reading and writing (multiple languages);

K. Science (theory & applications) and engineering;
L. Health and Nature;
M. Physical Education.

VI. Ages **fourteen through nineteen (5 years)**--secondary Education:
A. Core curriculum
    i. World Literature (multiple languages);
    ii. Mathematics;
    iii. Science and engineering;
    iv. Computer programing;
    v. Control Dynamics;
    vi. History, Geography, and Economics;
    vii. Life Planning (including parenting);
    viii. Physical Education;
    ix. Health and Nature
B. Elective curriculum
    i. STEM applications;
    ii. Arts applications;
    iii. Humanities applications.
C. Secondary thesis;
    i. A personally relevant written data-based study or organized portfolio;
    ii. Oral defense;
    iii. Publication.
D. One year field apprenticeship/Civic work;
E. Optional transition to higher education exam (only for those stu-

dents who aspire to enroll in higher education).

The School of the Future

In addition to earning a diploma, completion of this secondary education program will also give students a license to practice a profession consistent with their interests and life plan, like "electrician," "cook," "cosmetologist," "computer programmer," "robotics technician," "plumber," "nurse," "engineer," "graphics designer," draftsman," "carpenter," "mechanic," "office manager," "book-keeper," "health care technician," or any other profession you may imagine to be necessary in the future or at the present, which now requires two to four years of college.

The curriculum outlined above is not different from official curricula implemented throughout the world today in the way it describes or defines fields of knowledge such as "Mathematics," "Science," or "History." But the sharing of some of those labels and jargon may be as far as the similarities go between the curriculum of the past and the curriculum of the future.

In the last thirteen years working as a school psychologist in high schools I have encountered a significant number of students who don't like school, have no interest in coming to school, and become a source of distress and distraction to teachers and other students. This fifteen to twenty percent of the student population (in my estimation) becomes a serious discipline problem for school administrators and mobilize and occupy an estimated seventy to ninety percent of all noninstructional stuff, including psychologists, social workers, counselors, security, and discipline staff.

Even though most of these students have been identified in elementary school as having a learning disability, Attention Deficit Hyperactivity Disorder (ADHD), emotional disability, or some other brain-based disability, the reality is that some of these disaffected and at risk teenagers come from emotionally deprived and unstable homes that do not support the student's educational needs, do not understand or perceive the value of education, and are often disconnected from school or the educational process. In other cases, at least one of the parents seems to be involved and to care about school, but the student shows no motivation or interest in applying effort and doing well academically.

Regardless of why students fail to learn in high school, the curriculum of today has embarked on the idea that every high school graduate is going to go to college and succeed. From "No Child Left Behind" to "Race to the Top" our national educational policy of the last two decades or so has been focused on academic standards and the improvement and "refinement" of group achievement test scores. The "teaching to the test" phenomenon has become the greatest nightmare for teachers across the nation and has removed spontaneity and grace from the classroom. In my opinion, the true victims of this process (which eventually led to the imposition of a "common core" curriculum without a national debate on content and PARCC testing) are these disaffected students who are not interested, motivated, or prepared to embrace academics and the prospect of attending college.

It seems that the reaction to the "Nation at Risk" report (United States National Commission on Excellence in Education, 1983) led to a wrong turn in educational policy, which brought us down the path we are still following today.

Neither the common core curriculum nor the regimented testing that goes with it represent, address, or support the educational and transitional needs of these secondary education students who find no use for school as we present it to them. As educators, we often blame those same students for not taking advantage of school and for their own failure.

In my modest view, based on what I have seen through my work, the root cause of this serious crisis that is brewing in American high schools resides in the gradual disappearance of hands-on vocational classes and programs designed for students who don't find control in academics (e.g., literature, history, or algebra) and fail to realize they have valued talents that can prepare them for life and launch them to independence and dignity.

In part at least because of the unrealistic expectation that everyone will go to college, many of these youth, both male and female, exit secondary education with no skills, no self-esteem, no viable transitional plan, and emptiness of character instead of a robust values set to guide their future. Eventually, many end up at the state penitentiary instead of at the state university.

Furthermore, these at-risk and failing young men and women are often advised and encouraged to register in and pursue courses of study in the so called postsecondary trade schools and vocational institutes, where in some cases they are pushed into debt or outright taken advantage of financially.

In the future, I envision a school without tests, grades, or scores for the purpose of discriminating and ranking students on "academic" worthiness. Test-like exercises may be used as instruments of practicing and learning. All students will be rated equally worthy of accessing educational resources through secondary education. Any and all differentiation both in terms of instruction and of achieved skills will integrate the student's profile as qualitative descriptions of relative strengths and weaknesses that will be used only for the purpose of enhancing the student's potential for his or her life plan success, happiness, and wellbeing.

Education will be conceived, addressed, and implemented as a function of the individual's life plan, which begins in pre-school and remains fluid and flexible to the end of the individual's life. Instruction and the learning process will not be departmentalized by subject as it is in American high schools today, but will be done instead as a holistic integrated framework of understanding resembling the way events and processes flow in real life. That is how we learn to walk, talk, and assimilate a culture. We learn by observing, doing, and "documenting" in a way that makes sense to us.

The Explanation of Behavior: A Control Theory
of Everything

An example of a weekly lesson plan at the elementary school level would be:

A. **Monday--The class as a group decides on what project to undertake this week**. Guided by a supportive, knowledgeable, and highly motivated teacher, the class democratically and consensually decides what the project will be. This requires a nomination process, discussion of nominated ideas, and development of a simple practical action plan. This phase of the project will consider aspects of importance, relevance, and priority, such as societal, human, ethical, legal, and environmental impact implications. Individual students and subgroups within the class will use verbal, written, and visual spatial skills to present, discuss and support their ideas. They will rely on control dynamics tools such as logic, persuasion, clarity, parsimony, and flexibility of thought to make, share, accommodate, and evaluate their own individual ideas as they merge into one single project.

B. **Tuesday---The class will research and educate itself about the project at hand**. Let's say that the class has decided to build a dog house. Students will research available relevant sources online and in the immediate environment (the community). Students will break in cooperative units to cover all aspects of doghouse design and construction. They will gather data and information about the worldwide history of dog houses, including the first dog house ever identified as such, types and styles of dog houses, materials that have been used to construct them, countries and specific places in the History of mankind where dog houses played important roles in peoples' lives, dimensions, structure (engineering), appearance, and other architectural aspects of dog houses, such as their expected longevity. Students will go out into the community interviewing people and collecting images and artifacts. By the end of the school day, students will have organized all their data in simple multimedia presentation format easy to access and review. They will learn and share data collection methods and formats.

C. **Wednesday—The class will review the data collected on Tuesday, select and design a specific doghouse to be constructed, and obtain the necessary materials and tools**. They will use arithmetic, geometry, trigonometry, and graphics design skills. When it comes to materials, these students will learn and practice concepts of permeability, porosity, ductility, conductivity, hardness, shock resistance, transparency, and the like. All these decisions and processes will be accomplished democratically and consensually within the class. The teacher's role is that of facilitator, clarifier, and supporter. He or she will use his or her knowledge to explain why things work or don't work and will share what he or she knows with the students. The teacher will always have the last word if needed. But he or she will interfere as little as possible with the direction and flow of the project. The teacher will always make sure that all students have access to and participate in the ongoing process.

D. **Thursday--The class will actually construct the dog house.** With the support and help from their teacher, the class will apply their individual skills, talents, and areas of strength to actually build the doghouse, putting to use all their hard work and cooperation from the previous three days.

E. **Friday--The class will review the entire weekly project**. Each student will talk to the class about the meaning of their experience and about what they have learned. The role of the teacher will be crucial in helping the students conceptually organize what they learned according to the nomenclature of the branches and fields of knowledge. At the end of the school day the teacher will tell the students he/she would like each of them to read a book about dogs over the weekend, if they can. It could be any book in any genre or format (e.g., novel, poetry, nonfiction, essay, in any language they could read). Next week's project would be inspired by their weekend reading.

In the school of the future, teaching will be recognized as the most important of all professions. Teachers will be generalists, not specialists. They will be the smartest, most well versed in control dynamics individuals, and most gifted in flexibility of thought and ability to motivate others. Teachers will have an uplifting ability to infuse and spin humor and a positive outlook into anything and everything they teach.

Such teachers already exist today, unrecognized, underpaid and likely ignored and forgotten by society, but we all know who they are, and we know the difference they have made in our lives. I am thinking of Professor Amilcar Quaresma, my favorite high school teacher, a man who died without ever knowing the profound positive impact he had on me, one of his many thousands of students over the years. In the future, however, these outstanding individuals will be the heroes of society--the most-honored, highest-valued, and best-appreciated and "compensated" members of society. Not CEOs, not bureaucrats or politicians, not football players or musicians. Some of these "geniuses" we revere today may be equally admired in the future, but only because they chose to teach, and therefore share and apply their talent to teaching. Teaching will attract the best in us and the best of us.

For practical reasons, knowledge will continue to be organized under general content categories (e.g., astronomy, psychology, and chemistry), but the teaching of these different areas of knowledge will be implemented as an integrated process. Students will be highly motivated learners and they will learn through doing, collaborating, and participating in what they like and excites them.

Even though the university will be absolutely free to anyone attending, not all high school students will automatically transition or be expected to transition to the university. While completion of secondary education through age nineteen is expected and encouraged for all, students need to be recommended by at least three secondary education teachers and pass the admission exam in order to be admitted as matriculated students at the university. There will be no financial barriers to university access. This admission exam will be the only test with a significant impact on the direction of their future they will ever have to take in their career as students.

It should be noted that in the future, the concept of a salary, or how much money a person makes for a certain period of time (e.g., dollars per hour, or thousands of dollars per year) will not be affected by whether or not a person has a university degree. This means that there will be no material incentive in attending or graduating from college, other than the desire and ability to learn, teach, and contribute to the body of knowledge through original research, publishing, and other creative processes at the highest level. Graduate school, including what we call today the professional schools (e.g., medical, law, and engineering schools) will be absolutely free to attend and accessible to any university students who have graduated from what we today call "college" and who demonstrate ability, passion, desire to continue learning and teaching, and who have a life plan consistent with such transition.

In the future any individual who is born alive will be automatically entitled to a lifetime access to free healthcare (including free medication) free education, free food, and free shelter. These will be the four pillars of Human dignity in the future universal bill of human rights (UBHR). Privacy, private property of personal material and intellectual belongings, and the right of parallel free entrepreneurship will be equally assured, protected, and dignified in the UBHR. In other words, if, as an individual, you prefer to "purchase" and drive around an expensive solar-powered Mercedes-Benz, instead of using the highly effective, efficient, comfortable, and readily available public transportation system, it is your right to work extra, or otherwise negotiate or barter your private car, assuming all inherent responsibilities of maintaining, parking, and insuring it.

Once you legally own this unnecessary material object, it is your right to have it respected as your private property. This will be true for all aspects of society, where a parallel free enterprise system will be available to those individuals who chose to work harder or extra in order to achieve control in their lives through private ownership of material objects, access to privileged private services instead of the equally available equivalent public services. If you prefer to participate in the private enterprise system in order to feel in control of your life, you are not to be discriminated against or in any way judged by your free individual choices. As the saying goes, "If that floats your boat," let it be... As long as your private activity reflects **your true extra input** of energy and effort and not the use, exploitation, or enslaving of other human beings or animals, or the use of public common resources for your private benefit-- **Corruption has no place in the Human society of the future**. The role of the truly democratic government is to facilitate, regulate, and monitor all Human activity within a robust and healthy control dynamics framework.

One political slogan of the future will be "CONTROL YES!!! POWER NO!!!" Or, as Nancy Regan would have preferred, in her gentle manner... "Say NO to power..."

It is up to you, reader, to decide what else should be included in the UBHR of the future. It has been a pleasure having your attention this far, and I beg your forgiveness for the many things we have disagreed on. I hope to live at least another thirty-five years not so that I can just write another book (I am planning on writing many), but mostly to see some more of the future that I have imagined since I was a child.

CONCLUSION

In conclusion, if you read my book this far, I admire your patience, tolerance, and flexibility of thought, which are paramount concepts in my proposed control theory of psychology, motivation, and personality — The idea of control dynamics embedded in everything we feel, think, and do. In this last chapter, we looked at some obvious and likely criticisms my proposed theory will be subjected to, especially from some of my academic psychologist colleagues, who are more accustomed to the status quo, pageantry, and rarely questioned hierarchic authority of the cathedra than to the heuristic and pragmatic value of independent thinking in a context of experiential parsimony and invaluable self-awareness.

We also looked at the unavoidable ethical, political, and "divine" implications my theory and ideas are bound to have on the understanding of the Universe we are part of — namely the proposed shift from a manlike conceptual God to a single science-based Universe God, which includes Everything known and unknown to mankind and in which you and I play the role of Subject-Observer. We also briefly addressed the "interference" of intentionality in the control dynamics analysis and predictability of human behavior.

We dissected the difference between **Control** and **Power**, a required differentiation in the understanding of my theory. We then looked at the crucial role of education in human society and the kind of transformational process that will be necessary to transition from the capitalistic-exploitative-consumer oriented reality of today to an ideal humanistic, altruistic, cooperative, and environmentally conscious society of the future, through the implementation of a control dynamics

The Explanation of Behavior: A Control Theory of Everything

based curriculum and the widespread application of control dynamics to all aspects of organized and interpersonal human activity.

Glossary
of
Concept Definitions

This glossary includes only those terms that are central to the understanding of control theory as the explanation of behavior and also of those terms that need to be clarified and redefined in the context of their everyday use.

Actual Control. Actual amount, quantity, or degree of control attained by an organism resulting from a specifically defined organism-environment interaction as objectively measured by multiple independent observers or by reliable non-living mechanisms. May also be assessed by subject self-report.

Attitude. An attitude is a cognitively available, off-the-shelf, set of data about a given situation. These data were arrived at prior to the current behavior or situation through assumptions derived from learning processes, past experiences, other cognitions, observations, and biological parameters. It can be said that attitudes are the result of beliefs about situations and how those beliefs set expectations.

The Explanation of Behavior: A Control Theory of Everything

Automatic Control. Automatic control is direct or indirect control attained as a result of automatic non-conscious or conscious behavior.

Background. Interchangeable with the word *Environment*, it is the context (actual or representational) against which an object or subject behaves or interacts with.

Behavior. Behavior is any tangible or intangible activity (or lack there of) performed by an organism (subject) or an inanimate object as a voluntary or involuntary response (resistance) to a segment of internal stimuli (stimuli generated within the organism), external stimuli (stimuli generated in the organism's environment), or a combination of both.

Cognition. Cognition consists of neurological processes (intangible behavior) leading to the organism's interpretation and understanding of stimuli (perception). In this writing, cognition is conceptualized to include all aspects of memory and thinking.

Conscious Behavior. Conscious behavior is any voluntary or involuntary behavior, which closely follows, in time and content, cognitive activity in the organism. The organism is aware of the situation it is in and has an ongoing perception (feedback) of the behavior it is displaying.

Control. Control is the underlying purpose of all and any behavior all the time.

The Explanation of Behavior: A Control Theory of Everything

Control Degree. Control degree refers to the amount, quantity, or quality of control idealized, perceived, or attained by an organism as resulting from a specific segment of behavior.

Control Dynamics. Dynamic interaction of Ideal, Perceived, and Actual Control as it affects, determines, and shapes behavior in living organisms, including (and especially) in Humans.

Control Striving. Control striving is the sustained effort and ultimate motivation providing purpose for all behavior in all organisms at all times.

Direct (Vital) Control. Basic type of control, which, if not attained at a specific optimal degree, or within a required range of effectiveness, can threaten the integrity of an organism as such (e.g., breathing, eating, and drinking). Vital or Direct control is usually achieved through immediate very tangible segments of behavior.

Energy. For the lack of a more scientific and proper physics definition, in this book Energy means Matter in a "volatile", highly unstable and transitional state. We don't know much about energy, beyond the descriptive analysis and application of its apparent characteristics. Whether you accept the big bang theory or not, we don't really know its origin. To know the origin of Energy would be to know the origin of the Universe. Regardless of how Energy is understood, however, **Energy is definitely at the core of all behavior** involving living and non-living objects. **All behavior requires a transfer of energy**. In English, the words "power" and "energy" are typically used as synonyms, but not in this book, where the word "power" is reserved to mean an unnecessary excess of control.

Environment. Environment is defined as any medium or context in which an object, organism or system develops and behaves; In this book the concept of Environment is interchangeable with the concept of Background.

Environment Assimilation. Results from an object or organism displacement of energy. Whenever energy is displaced from an object or organism the environment assimilates that same energy.

Environment Energy. The potential and available energy contained in the environment of an object or organism from which the organism extracts its own energy and against which the organism has to resist in its behaving (striving) for control.

Equilibration or Equilibrium. It is sometimes used in this book interchangeable with the word *Homeostasis.* Equilibrium occurs in an object- or organism-background interaction when the environment energy is equal to the object or organism energy. Equilibration is, thus, only a theoretical construct when organisms are involved. In practical terms, equilibration does not exist between a living organism and its environment, although it may exist if the object is non-living. As soon as an organism dies, the environment energy is equal or greater than the organism energy. The exact moment when an organism is dying would be the only possible moment of equilibration. But not even then equilibration would be possible, because death is, as discussed elsewhere in this book, a chemical non-momentary process (not all cells of an organism die simultaneously). One can visualize a flow of energy from the organism to the environment (environment assimilation) and one can also visualize a point in time when both energies are equal on each side (the moment of death). However, the flow does not stop until the environment is randomly in control of the interaction, when the organism has been completely assimilated by the environment and no longer exists as a separate object. In other words, the *figure-ground* contrast would no longer be discernible by an observer (not in a visual or physical sense necessarily, but in a behavioral or conceptual sense). It is impossible, therefore, to visualize equal degrees of environment and organism energy (it is impossible to visualize anything without the presence of a flow of energy, without the object-background relationship.

Feedback Perception. The perception arrived at via the cognitive processing of data, information, beliefs and attitudes that entered the organism's neurological system as a byproduct or consequence of behavior patterns that have been executed or observed not necessarily at the time the perception is generated.

Field of Reference. Field of reference is the immediate broader environment surrounding the object or organism, where exchanges of energy take place. The organism will always behave in relation to the field of reference, and behavior can be understood only in the context of its field of reference. For cognitively mediated behaviors, however, even though the exchange of energy remains immediate to the situation (in the form of neurological processes and activity), the field of reference may be broader in "space" and "time" than for other more tangible behaviors. The field of reference may thus be a representation of a field rather than an actual environmental field. For example, if a person performs a behavior in response to a thought, the thought is a representation of something that may be removed in "space" and or in "time."

Homeostasis. A homeostatic state is an optimal state of equilibrium that represents the highest common denominator in benefits and economy of resources shared by a set of interacting systems at the same or at different hierarchical levels. Sometimes used interchangeably with the terms **Equilibrium** or **Equilibration** in this book.

Horizontal Relationships. Behavior that occurs when objects or subjects of the same hierarchical level interact amongst themselves.

Idealized Control or Ideal Control. Specific control the individual would like to or hopes to achieve as the result of a specific behavior pattern.

Indirect or Exercise Control. Exercise control is all non-vital control. Segments of behavior underlying exercise control do not seek survival of the organism as a direct or immediate goal (e.g., dancing, painting, dressing, building, and playing games). Exercise control can be conceptualized as preparation towards a state of reassurance or readiness. Exercise control is delayed control, which is stored in the form of information and readiness, self-confidence, and self-assurance. Ultimately, all exercise control may contribute to or become vital control in specific situations. For example, the type of control derived from learning Greek, is merely exercise control. Yet, once the person possesses that knowledge or information, it can save his or her life when approaching a sign written in Greek that says "DANGER!"

Instrument Organs. Instrument organs are the organs or sub-systems of an organism where exchange of energy and resistance takes place in a given segment of behavior.

Matter. Matter is energy as such or in any crystallized form. Matter is all that makes the Universe. To say this is not to say that there is no such thing as anti-matter. If we can in fact conceptualized the "existence" of anti-mater (as in particle physics), that would simply not change the Universe, for if "there is" anti-matter, it is already part of the Universe. It would have always been. So, to make it clear, matter is all there is, including anti-matter, or any other future concepts.

Mind. Mind is the common designation or conceptualization of a thinking human brain.

Neuron Pattern. A neuron pattern is a constellation, cluster, or sequence of neurons within the nervous system of the organism. A pattern is recognized when the neurons tend to fire together, simultaneously or sequentially, in association with a specific segment of behavior.

Non-Conscious Behavior. Non-conscious behavior is any behavior performed via the activation of either very frequently used neuron-patterns, or genetically pre-established neuron patterns often basic to the maintenance of vital control (e.g., habit behaviors, autonomic, or reflexive behaviors), and of which the person or organism is not aware of or does not become aware of until they have begun to occur. Cognitions may mediate non-conscious behavior, but, when they do, the person is not fully aware of the cognition or the behavior prior to their occurrence. The non-consciousness aspect of this type of behavior applies, therefore, to the *initiation of behavior* rather than to the behavior itself. For example, if you catch yourself rubbing your nose, the behavior becomes conscious while it is occurring, although, in most likelihood, you did not begin by saying to yourself, "Let me rub my nose..." If the behavior is conscious all along, then, obviously, it does not qualify to be non-conscious.

Object. Any non-living object that is discernibly separated or conceptualized as being separated from its immediate, surrounding environment while interacting with it. An object with self-awareness is also a subject and an observer of the specified segment of behavior

Observer. Observer is the component of a behavior that witnesses it occurring and is aware of it (the behavior). The same organism can be simultaneously the object, the subject, and the observer.

Organism. An organism is an independent open system able to self-regulate towards an optimal level of achieved or potential control. An organism must be able to absorb energy from its immediate environment by means of active interaction with it, and must also be able to grow and reproduce itself directly or indirectly through some form of natural and spontaneous process genetically established within the organism species.

Organism assimilation. Organism assimilation is the result of environment energy displacement in a segment of behavior. Whenever energy is displaced from the environment in a segment of behavior, the energy is assimilated by the organism. For example, you assimilate a part of your environment each time you breathe or eat, or each time you keep your room temperature at a comfortable level by means of burning gas, oil, coal, or wood.

Organism Displacement. Organism displacement is the amount of energy displaced, transformed, or transferred from the environment to the organism in a given segment of behavior (during organism assimilation).

Organism Energy. Organism energy is the potential and available energy contained in the organism, which the organism will use to resist or impose upon (to behave) the field of reference.

Organism Resistance. Organism resistance is the process of investing organism-energy against environment energy through behavior. For example, the organism resistance that allows you to *stand* is just slightly higher than the gravity force that would make you fall should you not be able to resist.

Perceived Control. Control the subject perceives as feedback or self-evaluation once the behavior or pattern of behaviors has been executed.

Power. Any behavior in excess of what would be necessary to achieve adequate control in any one specific interaction with the surrounding environment.

Segment of Behavior. Segment of behavior is any arbitrarily defined unit of behavior (e.g., a complete *breathing* cycle--inhale and exhale; eating, running, studying). In common communication, behaviors are often described as action words (verbs) or words that represent strings or sequences of actions that are associated in time or space.

Self-Perceived Control. Self-Perceived Control refers to the amount, quantity, or degree of control perceived by the organism itself as having been attained by that same organism resulting from a specifically defined organism-environment interaction as measured by the individual's self-perception of the event.

Sensory Perception. The perception *perceived* by the organism (observer) when processing information, which arrives through one or more of the senses.

Situation. A situation is a specific set of circumstances in which a given segment of behavior occurs. A situation can be conceptualized at a higher hierarchical level than an environment, because the situation includes the behavior of the subject as one of its components.

Subject. One of the four basic components of behavior; any behaving entity (object) with self-regulation and/or self-awareness (self-consciousness) qualities.

Universe. Everything that exists, whether it is known to you or not, is part of the Universe. Therefore, as redundant as the statement may sound, it is important to make it clear that there is only one Universe, *obviously*.

Variable Environment. Variable environment is the part of the environment composed by organisms or otherwise self-regulating systems (e.g., other people, animals, plants, micro-organisms, and autonomous or self-regulated machines).

Vertical Relationships. When an object or a subject at any given hierarchical level behaves against an environment that is at a hierarchical level higher or lower than its own.

Voluntary Control. Voluntary control is any form of direct or indirect control attained as a result of conscious, voluntary behavior.

References

Allen, G. E. (1978). *Thomas Hunt Morgan: The Man and His Science*. Princeton, NJ: Princeton University Press.

Asratyan, E. A. (1953). *I. P. Pavlov: His life and work*. Moscow: Foreign Languages Publishing House.

Bandura, A. (1965). Influence of model's reinforcement contingencies on the acquisition of imitative responses. *Journal of Personality and Social Psychology, 1*, 589-595.

Bandura, A. (1966). Vicarious processes: A case of no-trial learning. In Leonard Berkowitz (Ed.), *Advances in experimental social psychology*. Vol. 2. New York: Academic Press. Pp. 1-55.

Bandura, A., Ross, D. & Ross, S. (1961). Transmission of aggression through imitations of aggressive models. *Journal of Abnormal and Social Psychology, 63*, 575-582.

Beck, A.T., Rush, A.J., Shaw, B.F., & Emery, G. (1979). *Cognitive therapy of depression*. New York, NY: Guilford Press.

Bernstein, D.A., Clarke-Stewart, A., Penner, L.A., Roy, E.J., & Wickens, C. D. (2000).*Psychology-Fifth Edition*. Boston, Ma: Houghton Miffin Company.

Brogan, W. L. (1991). *Modern Control Theory* (3dr

Ed.). Upper Saddle River, NJ: Prentice-Hall, Inc.

Carver, C. S. & Sceier, M. F. (1982). Control theory: A useful conceptual framework for personality-social, clinical, and health psychology. *Psychological Bulletin, 92*, 111- 135.

Chopra, D. (1997). *The seven spiritual laws for parents--Guiding your children to success and fulfillment* (audiotape). Canada: Random House.

Chopra, D. (2014). *The Future of God: A Practical Approach to Spirituality for Our Times*. New York: Harmony Books.

Darwin, C. (1896). *The descent of man and selection in relation to sex*. New York: Appleton.

Ellin, A. (May, 2012). *Can going without money hurt the economy? One man's quest to be penniless.* Retrieved from https://gma.yahoo.com/going-without-money-hurt-economy-one-mans-quest-211049892-abc-news-topstories.html on 5/4/2012.

Ellis, A. (1962). *Reason and Emotion in Psychotherapy*. New York, NY: Lyle Stuart.

Eysenck, H. J. (1964). *Experiments in behaviour therapy*. London: Pergamon Press.

Festinger, L. (1957). *A theory of cognitive dissonance*. Eavanston, IL: Row, Petersen.

Fiske, S. (1995). Social Cognition. In A. Tesser (Ed.) *Advanced social psychology* (pp. 149-194). New York: McGraw-Hill.

Frankel, C. B. & Ray, R. D. (1996). *Emotions and motivation: Foundations for an information processing theory of adaptive competence.* Retrieved from Http:/www.ome1.com/Emotion Adaptation And Motivation.HTML (5/17/2016)

Fresco, J. (1994). Designing the future. *The Futurist,*

28, 3-30.

Fresco, J. & Meadows, R. (2016). *The Venus Project,* from https://www.thevenusproject.com/ accessed on May 8, 2016.

Freud, S. (1896). *The aetiology of hysteria,* Standard edition, vol. 7. Hogarth Press, 1953.

Gates, W. [Bill] (1996). *The road ahead.* New York, NY: Penguin Books.

Glasser, W. (1965). *Reality therapy. A new approach to psychiatry.* New York: Harper & Row.

Glasser, W. (1985). *Control theory: A new explanation of how we control our Lives.* New York: Harper & Row.

Glasser, W. (1998). *Choice theory: a new psychology of personal freedom.* New York: HarperCollins.

Guerreiro, L.A. (1987). An exploratory study of home-school relations among Portuguese immigrant parents who have handicapped children. *Contemporary Education, 58,* 150-154.

Guerreiro, L. A. (1989). *A cross-cultural study of pre-school age children's self-efficacy/ competence in the goal setting process: Development of an assessment procedure.* Ann Arbor, Michigan: UMI, Dissertation Information Service.

Grover, A. (February, 2012). *Bhutan: High Adventure in the kingdom of happiness.* Retrieved From www . telegrapg.co.uk.

Haley, J. & Richeport-Haley, M. (2007). *Directive family therapy.* New York: The Haworth Press.

Heider, F. (1958). *The psychology of interpersonal relations.* New York: Wiley.

James, W. (1890). *The principles of psychology.* Vol. 2. New York: Holt.

Jimi Hendrix. (n.d.). BrainyQuote.com. Retrieved

April 3, 2016, from BrainyQuote.com web site.

Joseph, P. (Producer, screen writer & director). (2007). *Zeitgeist – The movie* [Motion picture]. United States: Zeitgeist Films.

Joseph, P. (Producer & director). (2008). *Zeitgeist – Addendum* [Motion picture]. United States: Zeitgeist Films.

Joseph, P. (Producer & director). (2011). *Zeitgeist – Moving forward* [Motion picture]. United States: Zeitgeist Films.

Kelley, H. H. (1967). Attribution theory in social psychology. In D. Levine (Ed.), *Nebraska symposium on motivation*. Vol. 15. Lincoln: University of Nebraska Press. Pp. 192-237.

Koffka, K. (1963). *Principles of gestalt psychology.* New York: Harcourt Brace Jovanovich.

Köhler, W. (1929). *Gestalt psychology.* New York: Liveright.

Konstantinides, A. (February 5, 2016). *Boy, 12, killed after running back into burning house to try and save his father.* In http://www. Daylymail.co.uk/ (Retrieved 5/15/2016).

Krauss, L., Holwerda, G., Holwerda, L., Spisak, J. (Producers), & Holwerda, G. (director). (2013). *The unbelievers* [documentary film]. United States: Black Chalk. Retrieved from Richard Dawkins and Lawrence Krauss http:// en.wikipedia.org/wiki/the_unbelievers . Retrieved on10/1/14.

Langer, Ellen J. (2009). *Counter clockwise: Mindful health and the power of possibility.* New York: Ballantine Books.

Lazarus, A. A. (1981). *The practice of multimodal therapy.* New York, NY: McGraw-Hill Book

Company.

Levy, A. (1954). Economic views of Thomas Hobbes. *Journal of the History of Ideas*, 15 (4), 589-595.

Lewin, K. (1939). Field theory and experiment in social psychology. *American Journal of Sociology*, 44 (6), 868–896.

Martin, J. L. (2003). "What is Field Theory?" *American Journal of Sociology*, *109* (1) pp. 1–49

Maslow, A. (1954). *Motivation and personality*. New York: Harper & Row.

Maslow, A. (1968). *Toward a psychology of being*. 2nd Ed. New York: Van Nostrand Reinhold.

Maslow, A. (1971). *The farther reaches of the human mind*. New York: Viking.

Meyer, A., Rose, D.H., &Gordon, D. (2014). *Uni versal design for learning: Theory and practice*. Wakefield, MA: CAST Professional Publishing.

Miles V. (2008). "Maslow's leadership legacy". *Journal of Humanistic Psychology*, *48* (4), 444–445.

Milgram, S. (1963). Behavioral study of obedience. *Journal of Abnormal and Social Psychology*, *67*, 371-378.

Miller, W. R. & Seligman, M.E.P. (1975). Depression and learned helplessness in Man. *Journal of Abnormal Psychology, 84,* 228-238.

Mischel, W. (1968). *Personality and assessment,* New York: Wiley.

Minuchin, S. *(1974).* *Families and family therapy.* Boston, Ma: Harvard University Press.

Montaldo, C. (Updated October, 2015). *Susan Smith – Profile of a Child Killer.* Retrieved May 8, 2016, from http://www.crime.about.com. The

New York Times Company.

Powers, W. T. (1973). *Behavior: The control of perception.* Chicago: Aldine de Gruyter.

Raskin, M. (June, 2011). *Masters of the Universe: Noam Chomsky on universality and moral platitudes.* Retrieved May 18, 2015, from http://www.ips-dc.org.

Rogers, C. (1951). *Client-centered therapy: Its current practice, implications and theory.* London: Constable.

Rogers, C. (1971). A theory of personality. In Salvatore Maddi (ed.). *Perspectives on personality.* Boston: Little, Brown.

Rotter, J. B. (1966). Generalized expectancies for internal versus external control of reinforcement. *Psychological Monographs: General and applied, 80,* (1) (whole no. 609), 1-28.

Rotter, J. B. (1989). Internal versus external control of reinforcement: A case history of a variable. *American Psychologist, 45,* 489-493.

Schioldann, J. (2011). "On periodical depressions and their pathogenesis" by Carl Lange (1886)". *History of Psychiatry, 22* (85 Pt 1): 108–130.

Seligman, M. E. P. (1975). *Helplessness: On depression, development and death.* San Francisco: Freeman.

Shellabarger, D. (March, 2006). *Moneyless world – Free world – Priceless world.* Retrieved from http://zerocurrency.blogspot.com/2006/03/my-summary-of-why-i-live-moneyless.html on May, 5, 2012.

Skinner, B.F. (1938). *Behavior of organisms.* New York: Appleton-Century-Crofts.

Skinner, B. F. (1948). *Walden Two.* Indianapolis:

Hackett Publishing Company (Revised 1976 edition).

Skinner, B. F. (1953). *Science and human behavior.* New York: Macmillan

Spielberg, S. (Director) & Franzoni, D. (Writer). (1997). *Amistad* [Motion picture]. United States: Dream Works SKG & Home Box Office (HBO).

Stemmer, B. & Whitaker, H. A. (Editors) (1998). *Handbook of neurolinguistics.* Cambridge, Ma: Academic Press.

United States National Commission on Excellence in Education (1983). *A nation at risk: the imperative for educational reform.* A report to the Nation and the Secretary of Education, United States Department of Education. Washington, D.C.: The Commission. [Supt. of Docs, U.S.G.P.O. distributor].

Wadsworth, B. J. (1996). *Piaget's theory of cognitive and affective development: Foundations of constructivism* (5th ed.). White Plains, NY, England: Longman Publishing.

Watson, J. B. (1930). *Behaviorism* (revised edition). Chicago: University of Chicago Press.

Watzlawick, P., Weakland, J. H., & Fisch, R. (1974). *Change: Principles of problem formation and problem resolution.* New York, NY: W.W. Norton & Company.

Weiner, B. (1972). *Theories of motivation: From mechanism to cognition.* Chicago: Rand McNally.

Weiner, B. (1983). Some methodological pitfalls in attributional research. *Journal of Educational Psychology, 75,* 330-543.

Weiner, B. (1985). An attribution theory of achievement motivation and emotion,

Psychological Review, 92, 548-573.

Wertheimer, M. (1938). Gestalt theory. In W. D. Ellis (Ed.), *A source book of Gestalt psychology*. London, England: Routledge & Kegan Paul. (Original work published 1924), pp. 1–11.

Whitaker, C.A. (1976). *The technique of family therapy*. In G.P. Sholevar (Ed.)(1977). Springfield, Ill: Charles Thomas.

White, R. W. (1959). Motivation reconsidered: The concept of competence. *Psychological Review, 66*, 297-333.

Wiener, N. (1948). *Cybernetics: Or control and communication in the animal and the machine*. Cambridge, Ma: M.I.T. Press.

Wilson, E. O. (1975). *Sociobiology: The new synthesis*. Belknap Press of Harvard University Press.

Wilson, T. (1978). Cognitive Behavior Therapy: Paradigm shift or Passing Phase? In John P. Foreyt and Diana P. Rathjen (editors), *Cognitive Behavior therapy: Research and application*. New York & London: Plenum Press. Pp. 7-28.

Wilson, G.T. & O'Leary, K.D. (1980). *Principles of behavior therapy*. Englewood Cliffs, NJ: Prentice Hall.

Wolpe, J. (1969). *The Practice of Behavioral Therapy*, New York: Pergamon Press Ltd.

Wundt, W. M. (1910). *Principles of physiological psychology*. London: Swan, Sonnenschein .

The Explanation of Behavior: A Control Theory of Everything